They Say It's a River

Other Books from Squill Publishing

Patrimonious
A dementia-fueled revenge thriller

Rockstar Nobody
Sex, drugs, rock'n'roll, and murder

You Don't Look Artistic
Words and images to feed your brain hole

Magnovi
Dark, high fantasy adventures

J.M. Lefevre, They Say It's a River
Love in Laodicea, Book One
Fiction, Young Adult
ISBN 979-8-9898005-8-2
25 24 10 9 8 7 6 5 4 3 2 1
First Edition
Originally published in English in Junction City, Oregon

© 2024 J.M. Lefevre, Squill Publishing

All rights reserved. This book or parts thereof may not be reproduced in any form, stored in any retrieval system, or transmitted in any form by any means—electronic, mechanical, photocopy, recording, or otherwise—without prior written permission of the publisher, except as provided by United States of America copyright law.

To my daughters, the five pieces that form my heart.

And to my wife, the love that holds us together.

Dear Reader,

I'm writing to you from my childhood bedroom. Though, it's not really used for that purpose anymore. It has become more of a museum to the past, with yearbooks, a restitched rug rolled up the corner, two orange tackle boxes, totes of old clothes, and boxes of pictures.

I wipe bits of dust off a stack of yearbooks that keep memories of younger days that I'm in danger of forgetting. The power of being here is almost sacred within me, this small four-walled sanctuary. Surrounded by archives of my life in brown photo albums, concert posters, and faded trophies, the visual is striking. The broad, winding thread of the family that formed me and original sparks of the passions that have transformed me to the person who sits here today. The only gap between them is time.

The ways and means of how we communicate has changed since the days I am remembering. The volume of modern communication has become an unending avalanche, inescapable. Yet, in the silence of this little room, the words that have resonated within me from all those years ago, like an old Victrola in my grandmother's sitting room, ring as clear today as ever. The simple talk about the bonds of family and the power of love–what the greatest example of it was. In those decades that followed, I sought my own loves, raised a family, and pursued my passions. Yet, it's funny how often the answers that we are looking for are found on the path where they began.

So, I extend my hand to you on this journey to a summer along a Wisconsin lakeshore in 1992. A look back into the past and words I can still hear, like Julie Andrews in that rich high-fidelity mixed with the crackles of the needle through the speakers, of love less hindered by the poisons of our humanness. A love to give away.

J.M. Lefevre

Table of Contents

Place in This World	1
More Than Words	5
Fast As I Can	10
Into the Great Wide Open	18
Bird on a Wire	24
Hold On	29
The Greatest Man I Never Knew	34
Forever Young	36
Two Princes	41
Shameless	46
Eternal Flame	51
Step by Step	58
Tom's Diner	64
November Rain	74
Born and Raised in Black and White	81
I Cross My Heart	88
Flesh N Blood	92
No Son of Mine	97
Love is a Battlefield	101
Fish On	106

Hold On My Heart	111
Just a Friend	115
Heart and Soul	119
Father Figure	127
Smells Like Teen Spirit	131
Man on the Moon	138
With or Without You	143
From a Distance	147
Nothing Else Matters	151
Are You That Somebody?	155
Centerfield	162
Who's Gonna Ride Your Wild Horses	169
Keep On Walkin'	174
Into the Fire	179
Long December	187
Show Me the Way	190
Save the Best for Last	196
I Can't Make You Love Me	206
One	210

They Say It's a River

by
J.M. Lefevre

Prologue
Place in This World

"'Love isn't love 'til you give it away' were more than just words to Momma," Leah's voice trembled slightly as she held up two gold halves of a heart locket. "They were etched on her heart deeper than the locket in my hand. They were her life, and all of us who knew her felt that love radiating into ours."

She paused, taking a deep breath. The sound of the distant river and a gentle breeze washed over her, offering a moment of solace that gave her the strength to continue. She turned away from those gathered, as her eyes fixed on the long Georgia pine casket that held her mother.

"Momma, it's days like this I miss you the most. When I was a little girl, I'd tuck my hand into your pocket, hiding behind you. You'd slide your hand over mine, whispering for me to put on my rose-colored glasses and reassuring me that everything would be okay. It still strikes a chord in my spirit remembering the feel of your skin when your hand slid over mine as I helped you wear your half of this locket for the last time. It was my last glimpse of you in this world-and my last act as your daughter. Your final touch would reassure me, even then, that it would be okay. In these moments of uncertainty, I yearn for your presence and that reassurance. When all answers seem lost, I know my thoughts and memories are all I have. I've lost my rose-colored glasses, Momma, and now I see the world as it is – so dark and full of shadows."

"But you'll never be a shadow in my heart. So, as I stand here today with so many people who loved and were loved by you. I'm not sure what words to say that haven't already been said by others so much more eloquently. And, as much as anyone

Prologue

here, I remember your dislike for goodbyes. You'd always hold each of us as close as you could within your arms and simply say, 'Til your love holds me again.'"

Tears welled in Leah's eyes, their sting a reflection of the deep ache in her soul. "So Momma, today I stand before you, filled with fear, but also with fearless love. I will always love you, until your love holds me again," she whispered, placing a single white rose on the casket as she turned into the embrace of her father.

Leah lay on her bed, tracing patterns on the ceiling with her eyes. The last of the guests had departed and she heard her father moving around downstairs, the occasional soft clink of dishes as he sorted through the casseroles, cards, and flowers scattered throughout the house. The blur of the past week, culminating in the graveside ceremony that morning, weighed heavier on her than the goose-down blanket that covered to her neck.

Her fingers touched the intertwined necklaces resting on her chest. Memories of her last day with her mother, their final goodbye a week before, flooded back–a bittersweet mix of pain and peace. Five long, grueling years had finally ended.

For Leah, the wake felt like an eternity. Exhausted, her body ached for a resolution that never came. People spoke of her mother's love and caring heart, a testament to her life. Yet, it cast a shadow that seemed to engulf her own existence. It held a gut-wrenching beauty–each story, each smile, each hug a duality of comfort and fresh sting. A wound that scabbed over, only to be ripped open again, denying healing. The stark finality was laid bare with each well-wish and embrace.

"Your mother was beautiful," they'd say. "Your mother was kind. Your mother was brilliant."

"Your mother was..."

Was.

A voice from downstairs rattled her thoughts.

"You can't let her just run wild. That girl needs structure," her aunt, Caroline, was saying, her tone filled with tight-lipped Lone Star judgment.

"Not now, sis," came her father's tired reply.

"If not now, when?" Her voice was firm, unrelenting. "From what I've seen these past two weeks, she comes and goes whenever she pleases. You need to move to Houston. Give you both some grounding."

Leah's jaw tightened as she rose, slipped out of her room, and descended the steps in silence. She despised her aunt–a fake do-gooder who thrived on controlling everyone around her, weaving them into her net of so-called propriety and rules that she expected the family to follow. She lived in a kind of self-righteous oblivion, blissfully unaware of how little her judgments mattered.

"She just lost her mom." Brett tensed his shoulders. "She's got a job, she's getting good grades, and with all we've lived through, she's been nothing but responsible. I'd advise you to stay in your lane."

"My lane?" Caroline balked with offense. "This is family, Brett, and that is my lane. I'm worried about you, too. Living like a ghost out here, either hiding at work or holed up in your room."

"I'm doing fine, Caroline, and so is Leah."

"Oh, I see," Caroline continued, her voice rising. "It's too bad you didn't take my advice six years ago. If you'd had a backbone, we'd be in a completely different place now."

Leah simmered in her skin at the bottom of the staircase. She remembered her aunt's coldness when her mother was first diagnosed, how she hadn't visited until her mother's final days, arriving more to push her agenda than to help. And she hated that her father, as usual, felt forced to respond, caught in Caroline's web.

"What's best now is for you two to live closer to family." Her long gold fingernail pointed at her brother. "Tomball is ideal and the Corkers' house is coming on the market soon. I could even get you a pre-option."

"We are not moving to Tomball," Leah's voice cut through the room, startling Caroline.

She whirled on her heels, her face taut. "That's not your

Prologue

decision, young lady."

"Last I checked, it isn't yours." Leah's eyes were hard and unblinking.

Caroline seethed with indignation. "You're going to let her talk to me like that?"

Brett stretched his worn hands on the counter. "She's right, Caroline. This is my decision–and Leah's. And I'd appreciate it if you could respect that."

"Respect?" Caroline's voice was cold. "Since the seventies, you've done nothing but forget where you came from, Brett."

Brett gripped the counter, his eyes narrowing. "Caroline, I'd watch your words."

Leah, her anger mounting, took a step forward, her heart pounding. Watching her words was the last thing she planned on doing. "I know exactly where I come from, and I know exactly where I'm going–and it sure as hell isn't Texas."

"Leah..." Her dad's frustration at both of them had hit the breaking point.

Leah snatched her keys from the brass-plated holder and headed for the door, her eyes never leaving her aunt's.

"Where do you think you're going? I'm not done," Caroline barked.

Leah held her aunt's gaze for a moment longer, her face flashed with anger, before spinning toward the door. "You're not my mom, and you never will be!" She yanked open the door and slammed it behind her with all her might. She dashed to her car, cranked the stereo, and sped off into the night.

Chapter One
More Than Words

The hot summer wind whipped across the Chilhowee ridge as Leah gazed out over the breathtaking Ocoee Valley. Below, the lake shimmered, and the blue ribbon of the Ocoee River snaked towards the horizon. Far off, a faint clearing peeked through the trees on a small hill. Sheltered by centuries-old red oaks, a peaceful family cemetery stood, meticulously maintained, a testament to the past cherished by the present. Among the weathered stones, a small, gleaming pearl-white marker stood out. Engraved on it were the words:

LISA ABHAIN CLOUD-EATON
1953-1991
LOVING MOTHER, WIFE, AND DAUGHTER
YOU FOREVER ARE OUR HEARTS
TIL YOUR LOVE HOLDS US AGAIN

Leah parked her car on a dirt road along the ridge and stepped into the wind. She walked with caution down the white stone path that led to where generations of her mother's family had been laid to rest.

Reaching her mother's headstone, she cleared the area before settling beside the grave, forming her words as she knelt close.

"Hi Momma, I wanted to visit before my trip. I know it's been a while, and there's a lot to catch you up on. Dad's been wrestling with all of it these past few months. The memories here are just too much for him, a constant reminder of you. He's been talking to Grandma Ethel and Aunt Caroline about a job

Chapter One

transfer to Houston to be closer to them. But Momma, I don't want to go. I'll be a senior next year and starting all over again... well, it scares me. You know Dad. Once he makes up his mind, it's set in stone. Grandma's flown out twice and it's all she talks about on the phone. I'm trying to get along better with Aunt Caroline but she hasn't changed in her attitude or her opinions."

Her expression brightened as she looked out at the water. "Dad's going to check out the Houston office and I'm spending June with Bonnie. I can't wait to see her again. They came down for the funeral, and it was so nice to see them. Bonnie's driving now, so some trips to the lake should be fun. I vaguely remember going there with you years ago. I fly out tomorrow, all by myself. It'll be my first solo flight. But hey, I get to fly beyond the clouds, just like you are."

She sat and enjoyed the silence and peace of the valley. Looking at the time, she knew she needed to begin her two-hour drive back to the city. Getting to her feet, she whispered, "I miss you so much. My love always, until your love holds me again." Placing a soft kiss on the cool stone, Leah offered a silent prayer before turning to walk back up the path and to her car. Atlanta awaited and she had errands to finish before her flight.

Jake sat in his room, packing for his trip, as he finished a phone call with his friend Allen.

"So what's going on for you the rest of today?" Jake stuffed some crumpled shirts into his bag.

"I'm taking Laura and my sisters out to the Breakers this afternoon. When's your flight?" Allen tossed a football in the air as he laid on his water bed.

"I catch a flight later today. My uncle picks me up around nine pm in Chicago, and I'll spend the night with his family before heading up to my grandparents on Sunday morning," Jake sorted a stack of clothes between two extra-large suitcases. He counted out what he thought he'd need: work clothes, casual clothes, and a couple of nicer outfits for church and any social functions his grandmother might drag him to.

"So, what's the plan while you're there? You'll be gone

for two months with your grandparents. Are your parents even coming up this summer?"

"They're coming up after the Fourth of July. Part of the reason I'm going early is to help my grandparents work on the old family lake cottage. I'm hoping they let me have the place to myself. We'll see if that actually happens." There was a hint of doubt in his voice. "You know, get a chance to hang with my friends up there."

"Friends? Interesting, you mean your grandmother's best friend's niece or something. You showed pictures to me . I know Laura would be less-than thrilled if I were going to spend that much time with some farm girl who looks like Jennifer Grey. If you and Marta are 'seeing other people' for the summer, does she know that's who it is?" Allen teased.

"Oh come on, Allen," Jake chuckled. "You mean Bonnie? She's practically family. Honestly, I'm not entirely sure we aren't somehow related. As for Marta, the last I checked, she broke up and traded me out for the Luke Perry clone."

"Wait, so you guys are totally broken up? Laura heard you all were just going to see other people over the summer, not that it was done."

"A little fact that Laura doesn't know is that Marta started seeing other people before we talked about it. Matt's a sly one, I give him that."

"Ah yes, good ol' Matt Click. How's Mr. 90210 doing? I take it you guys never patched things up over the winter league?"

The thought of winter league still kicked him in the gut. "He's got a flawless arm, but it's annoying that the guy I honed my skills with for years is who my ex cheated with before we broke up."

"At least you're going on this trip with no strings attached."

"It's pretty sweet." Jake dug around the closet for his Nirvana T-shirt and found one of his Reebok Pumps. Now to just find the other one, he thought as he surveyed the disorganized state of his walk-in closet. "Mom, Dad, and Kyle come out after the fourth of July for like a week or two and then back to the Old

Chapter One

Pueblo."

"What are you gonna do for four weeks, besides chase farm girls?"

"Dude, my grandpa has a list a mile long for that weathered cottage from the fifties. As for chasing girls, Bass Lake is barely on the map, but gossip travels faster than the cars going by on the interstate. What I'm really looking forward to is some freedom."

"I get that." Allen laughed as he wandered down the hall to check on his sisters. "Dad's back to driving long-haul this summer. As long as I'm watching my sisters and not getting into trouble, my mom doesn't care."

"I wish." Jake looked through the pile of crap he had pulled from his closet, finding another belt but not the matching Reebok. "Wish I had your luck; my mom wants a minute-by-minute itinerary of my life. I can't wait to break free."

"And go to…" Allen poured a glass of Crystal Pepsi and raised it as a toast to his friend in a stuffy tone. "Stanford."

"Shut up, Allen," Jake fired back. "You know I don't want to go there."

"Why not? Your folks are loaded, your college is paid for, and you'll get a job at your grandpa's company when you graduate."

"What if I don't want it?" Jake tossed a pairless shoe at the wall.

"I'd say you're smoking crack. Everyone wants that."

"To be told what they have to do for the rest of their life? Why would I want that?"

"Because it's easy." Allen found Nicole playing Mario Kart in the living room and cradled the phone on his shoulder as he decided to join her for a game, selecting Koopa Troopa. "My parents work their butts off to give us what we have."

"But they're always gone," Nicole quietly added to the conversation.

"I know, sis, I know." He gave her a side hug, setting down the controller after the race and heading toward the hallway. "That's the part you don't have to worry about, Jake, money."

Jake was quiet for a moment. "I guess I don't think of it that way."

"Yeah, man, I don't work at Fry's for fun." Samantha was in her room arranging her Barbies for tea. She raised a cup for Allen as he sat beside her. "I do it so if we have a bad month, we can have groceries and Sam can get her meds."

He gently clinked his cup to hers and savored his imaginary tea.

"Wow, I didn't realize it was that bad." Jake looked under his bed, hoping he would have better luck searching there.

"We do okay, and don't feel bad for us. Just saying you may want to think about it before you turn the offer down." Ruffling Samantha's hair, he headed back to his room.

"I know." Jake grunted as he felt the rubbery pump on the tongue of a shoe under the bed. "I just have to figure out what path I want to take."

"You will." Allen noticed the time on the Desert Storm watch his uncle had given him when he got back from Saudi Arabia. "You have a good trip, man. I need to get my sisters ready or Laura's gonna wonder what I'm doing."

"Thanks, you too." Jake hung up the phone as he pulled the Reebok pump out from under the bed and tossed it in the suitcase, looking at the whirlwind of clothes around him. "Well, at least I'm packed," he mused as he latched the suitcases and headed toward the door.

Chapter Two
Fast As I Can

Jake held the payphone receiver to one ear and plugged the other with his finger so he could hear above the airport noise around him. "Yeah, Dad, I just touched down a bit ago, everything seems good for Chicago." His stomach growled. He had a good hour before boarding, plenty of time to grab some lunch, he thought.

"Don't forget to call Uncle Bobby, okay?" Paul reminded him. "And make sure you talk to him, no second-hand messages." He knew all-too-well the potential black hole of information his cousin's house could be.

"I know, Dad," Jake glanced down the corridor as the intercom squawked overhead.

"Maybe this time away will give you a chance to clear your head, help you figure some things out. And give your mom and you some much-needed breathing room."

"Thanks, Dad," a lump formed in his throat. "I really appreciate it. I'll call from Skokie later tonight. Love you, Dad."

"Love you too, son. Have a good flight." The line clicked as he hung up.

Jake replaced the receiver, a hollow ache settling in his gut.

Walking down the corridor, he stopped at the News Stand shop to kill some time. He saw a book his dad had been reading prominently on display, *Men are from Mars, Women are from Venus*. After reading the back cover and the table of contents, he was confused what all the fuss was about, let alone what planet women were from.

Wandering over to the fiction section, *Pelican Brief*

caught his eye, but a quick scan of the first few chapters seemed dull. He perused over a few more titles when a clerk placed three books on the Bestseller shelf. *Jazz* and *Waiting to Exhale* were both skippable in his mind, but the cover on the end read *Sahara* in a yellowed font over a desert backdrop. That it was by Clive Cussler sealed Jake's decision, having been a Dirk Pitt fan since reading *Cyclops* in middle school. A pack of Zotz and some Hubba Bubba rounded out his book purchase.

Back in the busy South Concourse Jake found an AT&T payphone cubical open. He set down his bag and backpack,as he fumbled with the Sprint calling card in his pocket and pulled out the scrap of paper with Bobby's number scrawled on it by his dad. After punching all the numbers into the keypad, the phone's shrill ring echoed in his ears.

"Hello?" a gruff voice boomed from the other end.

"Hey, Uncle Bobby."

"Jake! You having a smooth flight so far?"

"Yeah, it's good. I'm just chillin' in Phoenix until we board for Chicago. Thanks for picking me up tonight. I've got another hour or so before we head out, so everything's on schedule."

"Good, good, Christy and Jenny are itchin' to see you. Ready to ditch that Arizona heat?"

"You bet, I'm really excited to see you guys."

"Can't blame ya. Excited about spreadin' your wings a little, huh?"

"Yeah, something like that. Thanks again, Uncle Bobby."

"No sweat, kid. Call if anything changes. See you at nine."

"Thanks Uncle..." Jake started as the line clicked dead, leaving him staring at the receiver. He scanned the bustling terminal, checking his Casio watch. 3:00 PM glared back at him. Boarding wasn't until almost 4:00 PM and the departure board displayed a 4:30 PM takeoff. Time for a walk around the concourse, he decided. Sunset Bar & Grill beckoned – a burger and a Dr. Pepper seemed like the perfect pre-flight fuel. He settled in, watching planes roar down the runway as he devoured

Chapter Two

his medium-well burger, all the fixings except onions, and a mountain of steak fries.

Time ticked by. Around 3:40 PM, he paid his bill and headed back to his gate. A flight attendant, name tag reading "Florence," was busy with paperwork.

"Good afternoon," Jake cleared his throat. "I'm Jake Stanton. Just checking in before boarding."

Florence looked up, "Boarding pass, please," her eyes scanning the paperwork as Jake handed it to her.

"Jacob Stanton, connecting flight from Phoenix to Chicago O'Hare, seventeen years old..." Her voice trailed off as she reviewed the screen. "Everything looks good. Your seat assignment is all set, and you can even board early if you need extra time to brace yourself for the Windy City."

"Think I'll be alright. Thanks, though."

"No Problem! Just hang tight for a few minutes. I'll be making an announcement soon to get this Chicago-bound stampede started." Her eyes held a hidden glint of excitement as she thought of her own return home. "And, hey, thanks for flying America West."

With a nod of thanks, Jake went back to his seat. He unzipped his backpack, the familiar scent of leather and worn notebooks greeting him. Pulling out his trusty Discman, he flipped through his CD wallet, the worn Metallica CD catching his eye. Black Album it was, then. He plugged in his headphones, the comforting hiss became a shield against the pre-flight chatter.

Florence's voice crackled over the loudspeaker a few minutes later, her announcement about boarding flight 235 to Chicago O'Hare a welcome interruption. Passengers needing extra assistance, families with restless toddlers, and those with the magic of frequent flier status were called first.

Jake dug out his boarding pass, the bold '14A' - his coveted window seat. Soon, the call for rows 10-15 echoed through the terminal and Jake joined the shuffling line, a knot of anticipation tightening in his gut.

As he settled into his seat, the familiar outline of the Superstition Mountains greeted him through the window. They wouldn't be in sight for long. An older gentleman slid into the aisle seat next to him, briefcase firmly in hand.

"Afternoon, son," the man greeted, a warm smile crinkling clear to the corners of his eyes. "How's it going?"

"Good," Jake replied politely. "Heading to Chicago for business?"

"Yup, though I might sneak out of a meeting early to catch the White Sox game. A's versus Sox, you follow baseball?"

"Absolutely, sir." A flicker of amusement crossed the man's face.

"No need for the 'sir,'" he extended a calloused hand. "Call me Dale. You are a baseball fan yourself, then?"

"Huge fan, saw the A's in spring training back in Tucson. Even got to see Jose Canseco and Mark McGwire hit some monster homers. Met Jose's twin brother Ozzie too – super nice guy."

Dale's eyes lit up. "That's fantastic, son. I actually met McGwire myself at an event in Phoenix a while back. And speaking of..." he reached into his briefcase, a flourish in his movements. Out came a crisp baseball card in a hard plastic holder, the familiar blue border and crisp white corners were perfect. "1985 Mark McGwire rookie card," he showed the card with the inscription on the front reading "To Dale, Mark McGwire."

Jake's breath caught in his throat. "Wow!"

"They're having an amazing season this year. Bit of luck, a couple of solid hitters and pitchers – you know the drill."

The captain's voice interrupted to fill the cabin with the announcement of their imminent taxi to the runway.

"Well, Jake," Dale settled back in his seat, "Hopefully we have a smooth flight. Thinking of taking a nap, myself. Got the latest Sporting News here if you'd like some reading material."

Jake accepted the newspaper, carefully folding it and tucking it into the seat pocket in front of him. The plane roared down the runway, the familiar thrumming a lullaby in his ears. Dale was already lost in sleep not long after takeoff. Jake thumbed through the "Sporting News" as he slipped on his headphones,

Chapter Two

the pounding rhythm of Metallica drowning out the world. The names and stats soon blurred together until his eyelids drooped shut, succumbing to the lull of the airplane's engine.

A gentle tap on his arm roused him from his slumber. Florence stood in the aisle, a kind smile on her face.

"Time to stow your headphones. We're preparing for landing soon. Adjust your seat and get comfortable."

He glanced out the window. Below, the Chicago lights stretched towards the inky line of Lake Michigan between the clouds. As the city grew closer, Jake handed the Sporting News back to Dale and put away his Discman. He wondered what awaited him in the coming days. It was a question that hung heavy in the air. The landing was as smooth as it could be for O'Hare. As they taxied to the terminal, Jake glanced out into the city night.

"Enjoy your trip, Jake," Dale said as he grabbed his briefcase to get up from his seat once they'd come to a stop.

"You too, Dale, hope you get to see the A's game."

"So do I, Jake, so do I," he nodded and headed up the aisle of the plane.

Jake stepped out into the aisle and, after the usual dance of deplaning passengers, made his way through the jetway and into the bustling concourse. A familiar figure stood out amidst the crowd – his Uncle Bobby, sporting his usual tan jacket and a mix of gray and black hair poking out under his Cubs hat. Beside him, Jenny, now twelve, stood grinning widely with her wild shoulder-length brown hair cascading down a jean jacket over an oversized Bulls T-shirt and matching leggings. She'd grown so much in the last year that he hardly recognized her.

"Hey ya, Jake," Bobby gripped his nephew into a hug.

"Hi, Bobby." After he turned to Jenny. "Hi Jenny, you look as pretty as ever!" He pulled her into a hug.

"Hi, Jake. Thanks," a slight blush crept up her cheeks. "Do you like my jacket? I just got these patches put on it."

"It looks really rad." he grinned back at her.

As they headed to the baggage claim, Bobby turned to Jake, "So what are we looking for?"

Fast As I Can

"Two giant brown Samsonite suitcases,"

"Wow, glad I brought the minivan. Did you manage to fit the kitchen sink in there, too?" He teased as they wrestled the hefty suitcases off the conveyor belt and onto the floor.

"Pretty close. I'm here for two months, Mom wanted to make sure I had enough for everything."

By the time they had made their way to the van and got it loaded, a light rain had begun to fall. As they navigated the familiar streets of Skokie, Jake enjoyed the brief silence, his gaze drawn south towards the city lights shimmering faintly through the clouds.

"Not much of a view tonight," Bobby remarked. "But tomorrow morning, before we head north, you might get a good one.

They pulled up to a small split-level house on Williamsburg Road. Bobby parked and he and Jake unloaded the luggage as the rain began to pick up. Entering through the garage, they made their way to the laundry room when Christy called up from the basement in her strong Minnesota accent.

"Jacob, how are you, dear?" She appeared at the top of the stairs. "Got your bed all set up downstairs. Fresh sheets and a warm blanket to keep you cozy."

"Thank you, Aunt Christy." He gave her a big hug, getting lost for a minute in her Farah Fawcett hairstyle, its feathered layers a testament to a bygone era and the beauty that she'd once held. "I hardly recognized Jenny," he teased his cousin.

"Oh, don't I know," Christy laughed, reaching for her daughter, who desperately tried to slink away from the conversation. "Gonna have to get a pack of alligators and a moat if she gets any prettier."

"Mom, seriously?" Jenny pleaded, hurrying off to her room.

"Are you hungry? Do you need anything to eat?" Christy inquired.

Jake's stomach rumbled after a busy day of travel, "I could eat something if it's not too much trouble."

Bobby rolled his eyes as his wife took the comment as

Chapter Two

a personal challenge. "Want some pizza? I think we have some leftover Uno's in the fridge from earlier. You'll love it, really good pizza."

"Yeah, real pizza. The kind you eat with a fork." Bobby restated.

"Thank you, I can't wait." Jake took a seat at the table. Bobby grabbed himself a Miller Lite and set one down for Jake.

"Bobby," Christy began, a hint of disapproval in her voice.

"Christy, the boy's almost eighteen and about to head off to college in a year. I'm sure he can handle it," he argued then smirked. "Alright, alright, fine," he conceded, turning to Jake. "Jake, would you like a beer?"

"Yes, Uncle Bobby, I'd love a beer, thank you,"

"Here you go son, you're welcome," grinning ear-to-ear at his wife. "See, Chris, I have manners."

Christy mumbled something under her breath as she turned back to the kitchen to check on the pizza. She returned with a cake pan of bubbling deep dish.

The three chatted for a while before Jenny emerged in a long nightgown, fearing she might miss out on something. "What are you eating?"

"Just reheated some pizza for Jake," Bobby looked toward his daughter. "Then we're all heading to bed. Are you still hungry?"

Her look gave the answer as she sat at the table, though more craving the family gossip than the pizza

"So, what's going on out in Arizona that has you fleeing out here like a bat out of hell? I heard you took on your mother earlier this year and won. Hats off to you, man, that took some serious Balls!" Bobby gave Jake a pat on the back.

"Bobby!" Christy glared at him. "Please, Jake's going to think—"

"Jake ain't gonna think nothin', dear, it's okay," he assured her. "But seriously though, son, I'm not sure if your father has it in him to do that."

Jake dug his fork into the golden-brown crust smothered

by a mountain of gooey cheese, tangy tomato sauce, and savory pepperoni slices. "I don't know about winning. She got me kicked off the winter baseball league and I had to spend my weekends working on a community service project. The good news is I got to work with my Grandpa Clark and his friend who runs Habitat for Humanity down in Southern Arizona."

"That's good." Christy gave a look to her husband that signaled she would take the reins of the conversation. "Sounds like your mother is doing well?"

"Yeah, this year has been better, it's a challenge sometimes." He paused, unsure how much Jenny should know about his mother's struggles..

"And I must say, I saw that lovely picture of you and that beautiful Spanish girl in the golden prom dress. You both looked so cute."

Jake squirmed, searching for the right words for a conversation that he thought would never go away. "Uh, we... decided to see other people for the summer," he finally stuttered out.

"No way!" Jenny was shocked, "Natalie said..."

"Well, it's over," Jake injected, unsure what Natalie had told her younger cousin. He pivoted away to something else.

"I did want to thank you for picking me up tonight, Bobby, so I didn't have to get in so late in Milwaukee."

"Absolutely. No trouble at all. Need anything else before you turn in?" Bobby got up as Jake finished his pizza.

"Nope, I'm good. Thanks for everything. Good night." He placed his plate in the sink and headed toward the basement.

"Good night, sweetheart," Christy gave him a big hug before she and Bobby headed upstairs.

In the basement, Jake was glad to finally get to bed with some peace and quiet. As he settled in, unease gnawed at him, overshadowed by thoughts of what he had left behind in Arizona. The many decisions, unresolved, swirled in his mind as he finally drifted off to sleep.

Chapter Three
Into the Great Wide Open

"Thanks for hanging out." Leah stretched out in her seat at Gate B27.

Brett, still tired at 6:30 am in the morning, tried to focus on everything happening. He knew he'd be back at the Hatfield-Jackson in 48 hours, flying to Houston. "No problem, sweetheart," he smiled over the coffee he'd been nursing.

"Have fun with your cousins, okay? And don't give your aunt too much trouble." He wrapped his left arm around her and gave her a tight squeeze.

"Me, cause trouble?" Leah feigned disbelief at her father's comment. "I'm actually excited and looking forward to seeing Bonnie on happier terms and on her home turf."

"Yeah, well, your mom and Trevor were always close. Growing up, his mom missed the south and would come down whenever she could, bringing Trevor with her. Rumor is she has never loved farm life, even though that's why they moved to Wisconsin years ago."

"And, then, when he met and married Betty, your mother and her became fast friends, despite their different lives, they stayed close. As Bonnie was a few months behind you, they used to send clothes and things back and forth between you girls whenever they came down. I'm glad you all are still close," he added.

"I remember playing in the loft of Grandpa Eaton's barn, and being chased by that monster of a turkey the one time we visited before. I think I was six."

"Oh my gosh, I'd forgotten about that turkey! You're right, it was a mean SOB. You will probably get some time on

J.M. Lefevre

Into the Great Wide Open

the farm. But from what I hear, you might end up working at one of the family businesses."

The intercom crackled overhead: "Good morning, folks, this is an announcement that we will soon begin pre-boarding for flight 182, non-stop to Chicago, from Gate B27. Any passengers traveling with small children, children traveling alone, our VIP and first-class passengers, or those needing extra time to board, please come to the gate now. After that, we will begin boarding starting at the rear of the aircraft."

Leah checked her boarding pass: 9F. She began gathering her things and pulled out the worn paperback copy of "Outlander" Denise had loaned her. 'It's a beautiful love story,' she had promised the day before when she stopped by. In her Walkman was a mix-tape of her favorites by R.E.M., The Cure, Morrissey, U2, and even a little Paula Abdul. Her country mixtape was also on-hand in her side pouch.

Standing up, Leah looked back at her dad. "I love you and I'm going to miss you."

"I'll miss you, too. I'll keep you posted on what's going on in Houston." Leah looked away. "I know you're not happy with me about that, but please know I'm trying to do the best for all of us."

"I know." Leah hugged her father tight as her heart burned at the future that awaited.

"Now boarding rows 8-15, please make your way to the jetway to board," the announcement came through over the intercom.

Brett held her close, his eyes welling up a little as he looked into her beautiful blue eyes. "Til your love holds me again."

With a pang in her heart at his words, Leah whispered back, "Til your love holds me again. I love you. I'll call you when we land."

"Thank you and I love you. Be safe." He let her go and watched her walk towards the boarding line.

"I will," she called back, handing her printed pass to the flight attendant and boarding the plane.

Chapter Three

Leah settled into her window seat and put on her headphones, listening to the opening bars of "Losing My Religion" as the plane taxied for takeoff. Soon after, they were gliding through the clouds. Leah looked into the blinding blue. She leaned back as the gentle strains of Tom Petty filled her ears and before long, she was fast asleep.

Leah awoke to the excitement of a little boy behind her, "Look, Mom, you can see Lake Michigan!"

Wiping the sleep out of her eyes, Leah looked out her window. A vast expanse of dark blue stretched out as the plane banked. All she could see was sky until they leveled out, revealing the endless sprawl of humanity blanketing the eastern Chicago shore. The Sears Tower stood out above all the other skyscrapers–a giant in contrast to the rest of the skyline.

Knowing from her last flight to Houston that watching the ground rush by during the landing would make her sick, Leah closed her eyes as they began their final descent. She was grateful the pull in her stomach was short lived. With two hops, they touched down and taxied to the gate.

Stepping out into the light of the terminal, she saw Bonnie waving at her in an oversized Pink Energizer Bunny T-shirt and leggings and her "Aunt" Betty wearing a striped pink top and matching pink twill shorts.

"So, how was the flight?" Betty queried as they approached.

"Not bad. It was calm enough that I slept most of the way. It was so clear today, you could see for miles." Leah stretched her sluggish arms.

"What did you want to do today?" Bonnie asked Leah. "It's early enough and we have all day for sightseeing if you want."

"Hmm, I don't know. How about some breakfast and some art?

"What do you want to see at the Art Institute?"

"My big three would be American Gothic, Nighthawks, and the Seurat."

"As for breakfast," Betty chimed in, "We can find some

vendors by the park. How many bags did you bring for your trip?"

"I narrowed it down to just two. Can we stop real quick, I want to call dad and let him know I'm here." Leah turned to the wall of Illinois Bell payphones lining the corridor and searched her pockets for enough change.

As she rejoined them, she turned to Betty. "Dad told me he wired funds to Uncle Trevor just in case I needed anything."

"Yes," Betty answered with a touch of sarcasm. "You should be just fine while you are here."

Bonnie looked at the suitcases coming down the conveyor belt, "So what was the color-theme for this trip?"

"Bright yellow for sunshine and good weather!" Leah pointed at the first suitcase that came into view, a sunflower-colored bow tied around its handle.

"I want to see the fountain from Ferris Bueller, if it's not too far," Leah helped grab the second suitcase.

Betty looked at the large wall map of Chicago by the rental counters. "The fountain is just a short walk from the Art Institute and we could take a stroll along the lakeshore too." They were soon in the SUV, heading toward the skyscrapers of Chicago Loop.

They lucked out with parking when a Yugo belched out a cloud of diesel, opening a parking meter off Monroe. The choices from the local vendors was hot coffee, a small selection of donuts, and a blueberry muffin for Betty. They ate on the steps of the museum, enjoying the sunshine and catching up.

Inside the cavernous hall of the museum, Betty slid her arm around her niece and asked about what had been gnawing at her since the early conversation with Trevor that morning.

"So, Leah, how are things going in Atlanta? Are you and your dad alright? Trevor said your dad seemed pretty out of it on their last call. I know your Grandma Cloud is all wound up." Betty stood still and waited for an answer of more than blank stares. "Why just the other day, she was saying it feels like he was just walking away from everything to try and forget your mom altogether."

Chapter Three

Leah's expression changed, as she wondered how to share the feelings that had been on her mind. "Aunt Betty, I don't think any of you understand. When grandma came those different times to stay with us after Mom's stage-four diagnosis, it was helpful, but it was different for Dad. It was a long goodbye, an ending he knew was inevitable. He fought it, of course, but it was always there.

"He had time to prepare, but I don't think he anticipated the grief that would come after." Leah's heart stirred with the words she spoke. "The house has become a constant reminder of what we've lost. Every belonging, every corner, holds a piece of her life before cancer." She walked ahead to The Door by Ivan Albright. She took in the work and the nuanced detail of the painted wreath.

"Everyone talks about the grief of losing someone you love, but they don't talk about the grief of losing everything familiar. It's not just the person; it's the life you shared, the little things that connected you to them. The mug my mom used for coffee, the pictures of her and us on the walls, the spot where Pacha tore the rug that she mended. It's been seven years since she did that. The dog died two years ago and now mom has passed, but that line in the rug is still as clear in my sight as the day she sewed it."

They walked through the halls, admiring the remarkable works around them. Lingering to take in the awe-inspiring majesty of the Sauret. They sat for a while, captivated by its timeless, almost dreamlike qualities. Each brushstroke drawing them in deeper. As they moved toward the modern-art collection, Betty voiced what many in the family had been wondering. "I still don't get why you both are leaving."

Leah didn't answer, her attention drawn to Gilliam's Fire, its chaotic colored layers that seemed to glow from within. "The death of someone you love is like the lingering smell after a fire. The fire is out, the embers are cold, but still you can smell it. It's a constant reminder that it happened."

"Even years from now, I know that house would still hold that, Aunt Betty." Leah looked down as the sting of the memories flushed through her being. "That...That is why we're leaving."

Aunt Betty and Bonnie hugged Leah, folding into an embrace in a small alcove. After a moment of silence, Betty cleared her throat and looked at Leah, "At least you get to have a fresh start in Houston."

Caught off guard by the phrase, Leah repeated it. "Fresh start? People talk about it as if it's some massive gift. Starting all over, new introductions, new friendships. And yes, I know we have family in Houston, but they aren't close family. My Grandma and I get along, I guess. But Aunt Caroline and I, we don't. Her only goal is to have us all live together like she's my mom." Leah strode ahead, the anger boiling over.

Betty quickened her steps to catch up.

"Leah." Her hand reached out to console her.

She pulled away. "But she is NOT my mom and ain't ever gonna be!"

Several people stopped and looked at her. She put her head in her hands and sat by a Greek statue. "I'm begging Dad not to live near them, where I'd be the free nanny to my cousins. Because, I don't want that baggage." The fire that was kindling in her heart shone through.

"If I'm being given a blank page, I want to make sure that I am the one writing on it. Not some paint by numbers crap where the picture's already set. That's what Caroline wants to do. She wants to fit me into her picture. What if, that's not what I want. If I am going to write the story of me, it's going to be true to my heart." She clutched her Aunt's hand and Betty pulled the girl into her arms.

Chapter Four
Bird on a Wire

"Alright, let's go. Jake and I already loaded the van." Bobby called up the stairs.

"But, Dad, I can't find my earrings!"

"Then grab something else!" Bobby tried to stay calm and lower his blood pressure as he glanced at his watch.

"But then I'll have to change," came the strained voice from behind the door.

"Jenny, I—" He began, but was cut off as Christy spoke sweetly but directly.

"Jenny, could you come into my room? *Now*, please?"

Within seconds, the door opened and Jenny slipped into her parents' room.

"Why don't you just go tell them you're leaving and head to the van?" Jake suggested as he laid on the couch.

Bobby looked at the young man, bemused. "You said you had trouble keeping your girlfriend, Jake?"

"She dumped me. What does that have to do with this?" Jake was confused by what his uncle was trying to say.

"More than you might think, son, more than you might think," Bobby shook his head. "Hey, go grab those sodas from the bag in the fridge and take them out to the van for me. I'll be out there in a minute."

"Sure, Uncle Bobby." Jake grabbed the bag and headed to the van.

A few minutes later, Jenny came downstairs, smiling, two gold hoop earrings dangling from her ears.

"You look beautiful, sweetheart. The earrings make you look all grown up."

"Thank you, Daddy," Jenny hugged him and headed toward the door.

After another five minutes, Christy came downstairs in a purple drop-waist dress she bought at Marshall Field's. She had been saving it for the big family gathering.

"That dress looks amazing on you, dear." Bobby smiled as he looked at his wife.

"Really? It looks okay?"

"It's perfect. And today will go fine." Bobby pulled his wife close for a quick kiss.

"I hope so," Christy fiddled with her purse and got out a mirror. "I know the guys just pal around and drink beer, but the women in my family all gather to dissect the latest family gossip and reinforce their place in the pecking order.

"I just hope Aunt Edith doesn't cause any trouble. No offense, but your aunt is crazy as a loon." Bobby circled his finger next to the side of his head.

"Oh, don't we know it. But she's a rich loon and the last of the Glass sisters. My dad and uncles try to have her at family events as she's the final link to their mothers. I mean, she's almost 95. As long as she doesn't stir up trouble with Aunt Lucy, today should be just fine." She smiled as she squeezed her husband's arm.

"I sure hope so, or it's going to be a long lunch." He laughed as they headed out to the Grand Voyager.

There was light traffic that Sunday and, coming into the Milwaukee city limits, Bobby took the new outer expressway around the city to reach the Old Tosa village. On the run-down brick street, Bobby found a space not far from Church Street. They climbed out of the van and walked together to First Congregational Church. Rounding the corner from the top of the hill, Jake heard his Aunt Evelyn call out loud enough to make the passersby stop and look.

"Jacob Stanton, bless my soul, you get taller every time I see you! Hello, Christine! Robert! Jenny! Hope your trip up was good."

"It was fine, Evelyn." Christy waved to her.

Chapter Four

"Hey, Natalie! Natalie!" Evelyn looked around for her daughter. "Your cousins are here!"

A girl in a bright yellow sundress whirled around and turned, striding towards Jake. "Oh my gosh, Jake, I'm so glad you're here! There's so much to catch up on." Her giddy steps belied her self-consciousness.

Jake hugged Natalie, the obvious favorite among his cousins. "Good to see you too, Nat."

They all fell quiet as they entered the church for the service. The brood took up three full rows with Lucille Stanton front and center. As the call to worship began and the opening hymn was sung, Jake noticed the discreet discussion between his grandmother and the other women. They all seemed to nod in acknowledgment. Jake whispered to Natalie to ask what was going on.

Natalie explained that with a dinner for over thirty people about to take place at her house, Aunt Lucy was 'suggesting' that the ladies leave at the recessional after the children's sermon to go and prepare the dinner.

"Will they need help?" Jake asked.

"I'm sure, but I wouldn't dare interfere. Trust me. My dad will slip out of here as soon as the children go to the front anyway," she whispered.

As the organ played "Breathe on Me, Breath of God" and the choir and congregation sang together, the head pastor came down from the steps and soon called all the children to the front. Jake's younger cousins joined the other children and the pastor spoke to them about the message of the day before closing with the recessional for them to be dismissed.

At this time, all three of his aunts stood and walked out the back with the children. Jake saw his grandmother smile with a sense of satisfaction.

Jake followed Natalie and others to the fellowship hall for coffee, following the service. There, his grandmother found him and acknowledged his presence.

Jake stuck close to Natalie. She was his primary navigator in this world where he knew so few people, and Natalie had inherited her grandmother's knack for remembering names and her social savviness.

After they made the appropriate rounds, Bobby and Jenny caught up with Jake. He gave a quick goodbye to his grandmother and then headed with his uncle to the old two story farm house now surrounded by duplexes.

The kitchen buzzed with activity as the ladies worked on the meal. Jake noticed his Uncle Ron making trips in and out of the house to set the tables with various dishes and settings.

In the large guest room on the second floor, Jake unpacked his bags. This room, once the master bedroom, had become his domain for the summer since his grandparents lived downstairs now. Natalie, the second-oldest grandchild, had claimed her own space in a room at the far end of the second floor that had bay windows overlooking the backyard.

A few minutes after Jake finished getting settled, Natalie joined him in the sitting room, wearing culottes and her Gotta Have It t-shirt, having traded her sundress for comfort. The day promised humidity and the old farmhouse lacked central air, causing the two window-coolers to struggle against the heat.

"You gonna change so I don't look like a slob?" Natalie quipped.

"Yeah, give me a minute."

She continued as the door closed, "So, when are you going out to the lake?"

"I don't know; soon, I hope. What have you heard about me getting the keys?"

"Are you kidding?" Natalie tried to comprehend what alternate universe her cousin was living in. "Have you met my mother and our grandmother? Give you keys to a cottage an hour away, where your closest 'friend' is a smoking-hot girl who lives near said cottage?"

"Yeah, that's gonna happen right after my mom lets me go to The 41 for a double feature with Bryce Johnson on a Friday night," she snarked.

"Your mom lets you go to drive-ins?" Jake opened the door, now wearing board shorts and a University of Indiana

Chapter Four

t-shirt.

"No, you moron! My mother would murder me, and my dad would shoot Bryce."

"Yeah, that's...wait, are you seeing Bryce, isn't he our cousin?" Concern written on his face.

"Eww, gross, no! He's not our cousin." She answered quickly to distance the conversation. "We just grew up together and I guess they all called us cousins because they wanted that for family functions. One of the Johnson's did marry Aunt Alice's nephew, so if you are grasping for straws, he's like a fourth cousin by marriage, which basically means 'not related'."

"So, how long have you been dating then?"

Natalie stopped and gave him a look of death. "We are not dating! He's like family, that would be too hard to explain to anyone here. We just hang out. And Mom and Dad like him, it's..."

"Damn, it's a slick cover." Jake was smirking at his cousin. "You can't date till you're fifteen, per decree of your mother. But, hey, Bryce is family-but-not-family. You are too smart for your own good, Nat."

"I have no clue what you're talking about." A worried look crossed her face before she stared intently into her cousin's eyes. "But even if I did, I would suggest you not stir that up. I might just tell Mom 'out of concern' what I caught you and Ana Dahl doing in the boathouse."

Jake went quiet, trying to quell his cousin's threat. "Wow, Natalie, I thought we made a heart-promise that that didn't happen."

"I know we did," came a sassy reply. "But you rain on my parade and I'll send a flood on yours."

"Okay, I got it. Truce?"

"Yes, truce." She extended her hand. "Now let's get going and join lunch before my mom sends the spies up."

"Sounds good to me."

Chapter Five
Hold On

"Jacob, go outside and take a good look around before twilight hits," Lucy instructed. "We don't want Maggie getting into anything. And Natalie, dear, after you finish putting the food away in the freezer, see if Grandpa needs help putting the rest of the chairs and linens away in the basement."

"Yes, Grandma," they replied, heading off to their assigned tasks.

Jake scanned the yard, picking up any leftover trash from the afternoon gathering. Satisfied that everything was clear, he called up to the house, "She's good to come out, Grandma!"

A moment later, the pug came bounding past Jake, eager to explore any remaining treasures from the event.

Jake made his way up to the weathered back porch and into the kitchen.

"Thank you, Jake, I think that's about it."

Natalie joined them upstairs, with Alvin not far behind.

Jake headed into the living room. "Grandma, do you mind if we turn on the game while we finish the dishes?"

"I agree." Alvin settled onto the couch, reaching for the paper. "Let's see if Michael Jordan and the Bulls can win another one."

"That's fine, as long as the work gets done."

"It will, Grandma, don't worry." Jake assured her.

The television in the living room was turned on and the volume increased.

"He's amazing." Jake stared at the screen as Jordan hit another shot without even looking.

"That he is," Alvin agreed. "Like nothing I've ever seen,

Chapter Five

and I've even seen Wilt Chamberlain play live."

Alvin turned to Jake. "So, how was your season this year?"

"It was alright," Jake replied. "We made the playoffs, but we got crushed by Catalina, by one of my friends."

"Which one?" Lucy inquired.

"Matt Click."

"Oh, I remember meeting him." Alvin looked up. "His dad's your coach for the winter—"

Lucy interrupted, realizing winter ball was a sore subject, "Alvin."

"I know who he is, Lucy."

"Yes, I know you do, but maybe we could talk about something else besides baseball."

"It's okay, Grandma." Jake sighed. "His dad was my coach for many years. Matt and I are still friends for the most part, but we just don't see each other as much anymore."

Lucy, ever curious about gossip continued, "So, Jake, how is Marta doing? What's she have planned for the Summer?"

"Oh, Marta? She's busy working with her mom at the family construction company. As for us, we, um, we aren't really dating anymore, but we are still friends."

"I'm sorry to hear that."

Natalie was shocked. "When did this happen?"

"We'd kind of been growing apart since spring break. We officially ended things a little over a week ago."

"Ouch," Natalie cringed.

"I'll tell you more about it later."

"Sometimes that's how it goes," Alvin offered philosophically. "Until you meet the one. Just make sure she's the right one, before she clubs you and drags you back to her cave!"

Natalie looked at her Grandma with a humorous expression. "What? I thought Mom said..."

"I'll show you 'getting clubbed over the head', old man!" Lucy hollered.

"Just teasing with you, dear," Alvin gave a deep laugh.

Hold On

Lucy remained quiet, still staring down at her husband, who was clearly enjoying himself.

"So, Natalie, is your mom coming to pick you up or are you staying upstairs tonight?"

"I was going to stay upstairs and catch up with Jake tonight, if that's okay, Grandma."

"Yes, that's fine, dear. Just give your mom a quick call so she doesn't call me and we have a debate about who's coming or going."

"I will." Natalie left to call from the rotary phone in the bedroom.

Jake sat down next to Alvin on the couch. "So, Grandpa, what's the plan for this week? When are you planning on going out to the lake?"

"Maybe on Friday," Alvin thought for a moment. "But tomorrow, if both you and Natalie will be here in the morning, you could pick up your cousins and go. I'm helping out at the church with the treasurer."

"I thought you were retired from all that."

"Oh, he is," Lucy chided. "But your grandfather assumes no one is as good as he is."

"I am still a damn-good accountant." Alvin stood up from the couch to make a point.

"I know you are, dear." Lucy came by and settled her hand on his shoulder as he sat back on the couch with his crossword puzzle.

Lucy reclined in her blue-suede Lay-Z-Boy rocker with her book, "A Life on the Road" by Charles Kuralt. The pug curled up with her and they watched the game for a few minutes. "Alvin, it looks like the Dream Team is gonna wrap this game up. Do you mind if we watch Lonesome Dove?"

"I guess," Alvin answered, more involved in his Sunday crossword puzzle than the game.

"Jacob, could you give me the remote?"

"Sure, Grandma." Jake got to his feet as Natalie came back into the room.

"I think I'm going to head upstairs. I need to get my

Chapter Five

beauty rest. You coming, Jake?"

"Yeah, I'll be up in a minute." Jake nodded as she headed upstairs. "Grandma, Grandpa, thank you for having me up here this summer."

"You're welcome, Jake." Alvin smiled over his crossword. "Always glad to help you get out and spread your wings before they get clipped. And in my opinion—" he began, but Lucy cut him off.

"Alvin, the boy doesn't need to hear your opinion about his mother and his ever-so-lovely grandmother." Her dry reply lingered for a moment. "Jake, I'm glad you're here. Tomorrow might be a little cool, but you can at least get out and see the cottage and walk over to the beach. But, please, don't take the boat out 'til your Uncle Ron walks you through it. I don't want him to have a conniption fit. And you know the rules: make sure you pay Clara some money for the boys being at the beach. And if you do use anything in the house, make sure to follow your Aunt's lists for the A/C and the kitchen before you leave or your Aunt will be on you like white on rice. Got it?"

"Yes, ma'am." Jake kissed her head goodnight before heading upstairs.

Jake went upstairs and heard the stereo playing in the bathroom. Natalie was singing along to Paula Abdul on the radio. Chuckling to himself, he changed into basketball shorts and a T-shirt. He adjusted and crimped the foil on the rabbit ears of the old black-and-white television in the corner of the sitting room and reclined on the davenport by the bay window to watch the Bulls maintain their lead over Portland.

Bohemian Rhapsody was blaring from the bathroom when Natalie emerged in her giant neon-pink robe, stopping to turn off her boombox. "Bulls still up?" she asked, curling up on the right end of the long sofa as she dried her hair with a towel.

"Yeah, they're still up. Portland's trying to get back in the game but Jordan and Grant are matching point-for-point. They just can't close the gap."

They watched the game in silence until a commercial break came on. Natalie then turned to her cousin, "So, Jake, now that it's just us, what happened with you and Marta? I thought you guys were pretty serious. Like, I thought you said you guys had—"

Jake interrupted her, not wanting to discuss his love life in too much detail, "We did care a lot about each other. I gave a lot of things and so did she. And I thought it meant something, but I guess in the end, to her, it didn't mean enough." He fell silent. "I'll just say this, Natalie, as you start dating: a lot of people will throw around the word 'love'."

"Yeah, I know how guys are. Trust me, I've had some of my friends who 'loved a guy' who were dumped soon after he got what he 'loved'."

Jake was quiet as the game came back on. His thoughts were clouded by the memories of Marta. He looked over at his cousin and smiled, hoping to talk about something less painful.

"I'm looking forward to getting back out to the lake tomorrow. It'll be nice. I'm sure the boys will be excited to get out there. Have you seen Bonnie lately?"

"No, I haven't seen them since we went up in late April to get the cottage ready for all the summer company. She was over at the diner with her cousins. Does she know you are coming up?"

"I sent her a letter a couple of weeks ago letting her know I'd be arriving this weekend. What time is it anyway?"

"It's almost ten." Natalie yawned. "I'm going to bed, Jake."

"Me too." He got to his feet and went to turn off the TV. "Night, Nat."

"Night." Natalie headed to the back bedroom.

Jake started to get into bed when something caught his eye, a small oak box on top of the tall bureau by the window.

Chapter Six
The Greatest Man I Never Knew

Jake crossed the room, his eyes drawn to the old wooden box. He ran his fingers along its worn, grained wood, a familiar comfort. Carefully, he lifted it and placed it on the credenza by the dresser. The little number-combination lock made him wonder - had anyone changed it? Tilting the box, he noticed a single word penciled on the clean veneered plywood bottom: "Home." A smile grew on his face as he carefully spun the dial to 6-0-2, the area code of his home in Arizona. It made a satisfying click as the lock was released. Lifting the lid, a musty scent greeted him, along with a sight that always tugged at his heart.

Three sets of initials were knife-scratched into the lid: A.S. for his grandfather, P.S. for his father, and his own that he had proudly etched on his twelfth birthday. One day, this heirloom would be passed on to his own eldest child.

The wide-grained tiger-oak box had been a gift from Jake's great-grandfather, George, to Alvin on his fifteenth birthday in 1936. Inside, George had placed his WWI victory medal and dog tags, a crisp $20 bill, and the inspection card from Ellis Island, a memento of his own father, Charles Stanton's, arrival in America from Ireland with his family in 1887.

Alvin kept the box in the family safe, adding his own keepsakes: his Purple Heart and dog tags and a letter Lucy had written while he was overseas, before passing the box on to his son, Paul, when he turned twelve.

Paul's prized possessions, his teenage mementos - his Willie Mays rookie card, his Eagle Scout pin, and a ticket from the 1958 World Series.

The Greatest Man I Never Knew

When Paul left for college, the box was placed back in the 1920s iron bank safe in the basement. The summer Jake turned twelve, his father and grandfather took him to Uncle Joe's farm near where the original Stanton homestead had been, shared their family history, and entrusted him with the box. Alvin watched with emotion as Jake carved his initials onto the lid.

Two years later, concerned about the deteriorating wood, he rebuilt the bottom, adding a clever secret compartment with a special groove that allowed for access. This hidden space became the new home for his prized Willie Mays and Hank Aaron rookie cards, a gift from his father.

Gazing into the box, memories flooded Jake's mind. He wondered what treasures he would add for his future children. He closed and set the latch before placing back on the dresser. Climbing into bed, Jake stared at the yellowed floral wallpaper in the room and the windows that peered out at the city lights, his heart heavy with questions. He'd grown up with stories of his great-great-grandfather and his family selling everything, including their farm in Donegal, to secure passage to America. He'd heard tales of the journey and the struggle to survive in New York before heading west and settling in Wisconsin. He knew the stories of his great-grandfather in World War I and his grandfather in World War II. The Purple Heart he'd earned for saving two of his fellow soldiers in Germany. A sacrifice that cost him part of his left foot. Yet, his grandfather always said a life saved was worth any price.

And then stories about how his parents met in college around the time his grandfather was starting a new mining venture with two partners, north of the city. His parents had poured their lives into the business and his childhood photos documented his many toddler years in the family office. And now, almost twenty years later, their hard work had paid off handsomely.

But where did Jake fit in? This was 1992 and the July celebration loomed, marking one-hundred years since the first Stanton was born on American soil - his great-grandfather, George. With such a legacy and footsteps cast before him, what would Jake leave behind?

Chapter Seven
Forever Young

"Natalie, I have to pee," came Nick's shrill voice from the back seat of the Buick Roadmaster.

"Oh my God!" Matt exploded at his brother. "Didn't you go at the house?"

"No, You were in the bathroom and Jake picked us up early."

"We'll be there soon." Natalie looked back at him from the front seat. "See, there is the Orange silo, so like twenty-five more minutes."

"I don't know," Nick whined, squeezing his knees together

"Look," Jake pointed. "There is a McDonald's at the next exit, you two can run in there real quick, okay?"

"I want McDonald's." Brian poked his older sister.

"Don't you start that, Bri I helped Grandma pack this lunch, we all are going to eat it. You got it?" Natalie hissed.

Brian got it but wasn't happy. He slumped and frowned, arms crossed over his chest. Nick shifted in his middle seat as he tried to hold it. He disliked being the youngest because he always had to sit in the middle.

Jake exited the freeway and Nick scrambled over his brother as he followed Natalie inside to use the bathroom. Crisis averted.

They soon were turning onto County Highway 16 and making their way to the family cottage on the lake. As Jake pulled onto the small gravel drive he asked Natalie if there was room in the garage to park. Her laugh answered his question. Usually the oldest cousin, Natalie quickly took charge of the situation, instructing the boys to help Jake unload as she unlocked the cottage.

"No one makes a mess 'cause I don't want Mom ripping me a new one, okay?" She spoke with a tone that the boys knew better than to cross.

The air hung heavy inside. Matt wiped his brow. "Can we turn the air on?"

"I guess for a little bit, Matty, but don't leave it running," she nodded.

Jake headed upstairs to the bedroom to get changed, pausing to glance out the window at Bass Lake, below. The placid glacial lake was glistening as the sun's reflection rippled across the shallow basin. Back downstairs, the air conditioner was chugging along to cool the floor, as Natalie reviewed one of her mother's lists.

"Nat, do you think the boys are gonna want to go over and swim at the beach or just jump off the dock?" Jake asked as he entered the kitchen.

"They like the beach. It is sloped and shallow enough that all three of them can swim without having to worry about boats coming too close."

"Okay, I'll go across and say hello to Mrs. Beck and take care of us for the day."

"Thanks, Jake, I'll get lunch ready."

Jake headed out the door and across the highway to the local diner. The bells on the door jingled and, inside, the aroma of grease and sausages filled his nostrils. The Beck's was a long-time establishment of the Bass Lake Community. The family had owned the beach on the west side of the lake that adjoined the farm since the turn of the century. When the lake community began to grow in the twenties, the Beck's opened the beach to the public and, in the forties, a young Clara convinced her father-in-law to invest in a family diner. Its reputation for good burgers and famous pies were well known throughout the county.

The grilled burgers and french fries on the pickup made Jake's mouth water as he entered the dining room. Metal tables draped with plastic checkerboard tablecloths were arranged in the

Chapter Seven

dining area opposite the counter and cashier. In the back corner was Jake's primary attraction to the roadside establishment. Galaga and Centipede were set up on either side of the crown jewel, the High-Speed Pinball machine with gnarly effects, chaotic wire-form ramps, and engine-revving sound effects.

Behind the counter, a smiling woman in her late sixties was flipping burgers and giving orders to two teen boys.

"Hi, Mrs. Beck." Jake caught Clara's attention as he approached the counter.

"Oh my gosh, Jacob Stanton, I heard you were in town. I swear you get taller every time I see you." She walked around the counter to give Jake a hug. "So what brings you over here today? Alvin going fishing?"

"No, Grandpa's at the church and Gram's out at the farm with Uncle Joe. Just Natalie, the boys, and I." Jake glanced around the room. "So, just your grandsons working today?"

Clara knew the real question the boy was asking. "Yeah, just the boys are working today. If you're looking for my granddaughter, she is up at the house. Not sure when she's coming down. She's still getting her second cousin settled in after picking her up in Chicago."

"Really, her cousin? Where is she from?"

"Atlanta, she's up here for a month or so. It's a long story. Bonnie will probably fill you in soon enough. It was good to see you, I gotta get back to keeping the boys from running off all my customers for being too slow. Ten bucks should do it for all of you."

"Sounds good to me."

"If I see Bonnie, I'll let her know you all are here. You kids have a good afternoon. And tell Lucy I'll see her at the women's social and Alvin not to be a stranger."

"I will." Jake waved, heading out of the drive-in. A few cars were rolling up as he crossed the road and headed up the little berm toward the cottage.

Back inside, Natalie had lunch all spread out on the table. The air conditioner had taken the edge off the stuffiness.

"Thank you, Natalie, for getting this all set."

"No problem." Natalie was cutting Nick's cheese sandwich into squares. The boys were seated at the table and ready to dive into a spread of Usinger Sausages, cheddar and brick cheese from Uncle Joe's, and an open bag of Roundy's potato chips.

"Here you go, Nicky," she handed him his plate and sat down.

After lunch was finished, the boys cleaned up and Natalie put the food in the fridge. Jake made a mental note to not forget it, lest they tick off his aunt.

Natalie grabbed her bag. "Boys, get ready upstairs." She disappeared into the bathroom and, soon, she exited wearing a large oversized Ren & Stimpy T-shirt and sandals. The boys were all changed and started heading toward the door.

"Wait, sunscreen, all of you," Natalie handed the sunscreen to Jake and Matt as they started putting it on before helping Nick.

"Natalie, do you need sunscreen?" Matt handed her the bottle.

"Yes, Matt, thank you. I'll put mine on at the beach."

"Okay, does everyone have what you need?" Jake looked at the boys as he grabbed a cooler. Natalie opened the door and the five of them headed out along the road down to the beach. The boys went crashing into the water. Jake looked at Natalie.

"Want to take shifts? I'll keep an eye on the boys for a minute while you get ready but, then, I want to take a nap. I'm still fighting jet-lag and the time change."

"Yeah, that's fine. By the way, don't laugh at my swimsuit."

"Why would I laugh?" Jake looked up as he set down the cooler.

"It's just, I don't know. You used to always make fun of me when we were younger," she said, stretching the frayed hem of the long shirt with her fingers.

Jake put his hand on her shoulder and pulled her in. "Natalie, you are perfect just as you are, you shouldn't be so worried about it."

Chapter Seven

"Okay." She tugged at the hem of her t-shirt, glancing around before slowly peeling it off to reveal her yellow-and-green one-piece. She folded her arms across her stomach, shifting from foot to foot as Jake made his way to the water. As she applied sunscreen, her eyes darted toward the boys laughing with Jake.

After a quick dip in the cool water, Jake dragged a nearby lounge chair under the shade of an oak tree and laid back to catch a short nap.

Chapter Eight
Two Princes

"Leah, are you about ready to go?" Bonnie fixed her top and took another glance in the mirror.

"Yeah, almost ready." Leah looked back through her luggage, packing her bag for the day. "No swimming today, right?"

"No, not today. I need to drop off some supplies for my grandma at the diner. We can grab lunch."

"Do we need to take Joe?"

"No, Joe's staying here. He normally avoids the diner as he gets drafted into working." Bonnie laughed as they headed downstairs. A neon orange Post-It embossed with "A Note from Betty" was stuck to a box of styrofoam cups with a written reminder to grab lids. With the supplies loaded, the girls enjoyed the sunny afternoon drive to Bass Lake.

"So, how far are you all from the lake?"

"Like thirty-to-forty minutes. Not too far, but far enough. My cousins live just up the road, and they are always getting called to work at the restaurant."

There was almost no traffic on the old county road, till they pulled around behind the diner. As they began unloading the boxes, Clara swung open the backdoor.

"Saw you pull up. Thank you for bringing these over." Clara took a box and set it on the storage shelf. "Leah, I hardly recognize you. Come here, child, let me give you a hug. It's like looking through a time machine, how much you look…" Clara caught herself mid sentence.

"It's okay. Mom always talked about the trips up here in the seventies."

Chapter Eight

"How are you doing, dear?" Clara looked at the girl with warm eyes.

"As good as I can, I guess. Some days it's still tough." Leah looked away.

"I'm sure they are, dear. I'm sure they are." Clara reached out, giving her a tight hug. As she let her go, she looked at her granddaughter, "So what are you ladies up to today?"

"I wanted to show Leah our beach and grab some lunch before swinging by Aunt Ingrid's to let Leah catch up with the cousins. Mom wanted me to grab some more jams from the cellar, too," Bonnie added.

"Probably not today, Bonnie. Your Aunt has a doctor's appointment with Nole, and Rusty and Caleb are busy inside. It's the lunch crowd, you know."

Clara's eyes twinkled as she took in the broad smile on Leah's face as she talked. "What are you smiling at, sweetheart? You don't have many Minnesotans in Georgia?"

"No, we don't. I forgot how much I loved it. I'm so glad to be away from everything and just relax."

"With your pretty face and the sweet southern accent, you'll make some friends here at the lake and feel right at home in no time." Clara got lost in her thoughts before turning her attention to her granddaughter. "Actually, speaking of 'friends', Bonnie, that handsome Stanton boy is back in town and at the beach today with his cousins."

"Jake's here already?" She flushed with surprise.

Leah cocked an eye at her cousin, who gave her an "I'll explain in a minute" look.

"Here for the next two months, per Lucy. We've always loved how close you two have been over the years."

"He wrote to me that he was coming up this weekend, but I hadn't heard from him yet."

"Wrote you, now, did he?" A glint flashed in Clara's eye as she caught the glow in Bonnie's face. "Go over and say hello, dear. Then come back and get a bite to eat."

"Thanks, Grandma."

The moment they exited, Leah turned to her cousin with

a raised eyebrow. "Alright, spill the beans. Who is this Jake?"

Bonnie tried to coolly keep things under wraps. "He's my grandma's best friend's grandson. Lives in Arizona, but spends summers here."

"Hmm, so how close are you guys?" Leah pressed. "Is he hot?"

"It's weird." Bonnie's emotions were conflicted on how to describe Jake. "He's kind of like family. I mean, he's not bad looking. Tall, plays baseball, and has a band with his friends. You know, typical boy."

"Can't wait to meet your hot Arizona *'friend'*." Leah used air quotes for emphasis as they walked through the fenced gate.

"Shh, stop it! People can hear you," Bonnie hissed. She wondered in her heart how much to share with Leah. About Jake, their summers, and the gossip that carried here like leaves in the wind.

They could see Natalie playing in the water with her cousins and other kids as they walked past a group of local moms, who waved to Bonnie.

Natalie saw them and waved, then pointed to the sprawling bur oak by the fence. Under the shade of the weathered tree, a tall boy, shirtless, wearing blue board shorts and an A's hat over his face, was sound asleep.

Bonnie waved back to Natalie but put her fingers over her lips before she shouted anything. Bonnie motioned to Leah as they casually came up on either side of the sleeping boy. Bonnie leaned down 'til her lips neared Jake's and blew air across them, causing him to mumble something under his breath. Not done, she leaned in closer and blew into his ear, stirring him from his slumber.

Jake narrowed his eyes against the sunlight, attempting to loosen the haze that was clouding his mind.

Leah could no longer resist, "Bonnie, from your description of this desert boy, I was hoping for someone with nice, bronzed, LA legs to match those golden locks, not a blinding farmer's tan."

Chapter Eight

"Be nice, Leah," said Bonnie. "It's obvious the boy is sleeping off his jet lag."

Jake's eyes focused. Bonnie's bright face and her tussle of brown curls greeted him. She was wearing her standard tank top and brightly colored shorts. To her left was a girl he had never seen before, whose face belied a certain level of mischief brewing behind those blue eyes. She had raven-black hair that flowed clear to her shoulders as effortlessly as an afternoon walk, her attitude matching the tight-fitting 'Out of Time' tee and cut off jean shorts.

Jake tried to find words to say as his brain struggled in its half-alert state. He took too long for Leah, as her quick wit fired back at him. "And they say Southerners talk slow, Bonnie. I do believe I have found competition for the boys back home." Tossing her hair to the side, she gestured to Bonnie. "Is he able to speak?"

"Oh, don't you worry about that, girl."

Natalie, out of breath, dragged Nick closer to the shore, her voice strained from yelling at Brian to come to the shallower waters. Matt offered to watch his little brother while Natalie hurried up the beach to join the older girls.

"Hey, Bonnie, how are you doing? Who's your friend?"

"Hi, Natalie, this is my cousin, Leah, from Atlanta."

Bonnie ran her hand along Jake's arm, trying to get him to look at her and stop wide-eyed staring at her cousin. "When did you get in?"

"I flew in the other night."

"That's cool," Bonnie noticed his stare. Her skin pricking, she turned to Natalie. "How's the water?"

"Not bad. I was hoping it would be warmer today, but it's okay."

"How much longer are you guys going to be out here?"

Jake checked his watch. It was a little after noon. "Another hour or so before we head back to the city."

Jake drifted back to the girl with the haunting, glacial blue eyes, "So, how long are you staying in Wisconsin?"

"And why would that interest you, Farmer Tan?" Leah

teased. "I've got four weeks before my party gets crashed, so I'll be around." Jake leaned in, trying to act cool. "Just curious if I'd be seeing you again."

Natalie rolled her eyes. "It was wonderful to see you, Bonnie. Nice to meet you, Leah. I'm going to head back out and swim with the boys."

"Nice to meet you, Natalie."

"See you later, kiddo," Bonnie waved as Natalie bounded back out to the water. "So Jake, did you guys already have lunch?"

"At the cottage. Why?"

"We were going to hang out at the diner for a bit and have some burgers. If you want to stop by, my mom just updated the jukebox. They might even have some songs you country-folk like." She took a playful lean into Jake's shoulder before they headed toward the gate.

"Well, I might just have to check that out," He called back, his eyes following the girls as they crossed the road and slipped back into the diner.

Chapter Nine
Shameless

"Hey, Nat." Jake called out to her in the water.

"What, Jake?" Natalie looked up as she adjusted Nick's floating ring.

"How much longer do you think you wanna be in the water? Maybe you and the boys should take a break?"

"Why?" Natalie glanced back to check on how far out Matt had gone to the buoys.

Jake looked across the highway. "Maybe I want to go across to the diner."

Her eyes narrowed with her dry reponse. "Why?"

"You know…" His voice trailed off as he went down to the shore, hoping Natalie would catch his drift.

"We've already had lunch, Jake, and I don't think we have enough cash to buy more food for all of us, unless you have more with you." She waded up to the shore, so as not to shout. "I mean, I guess we could take a break if you give me a minute. I need to get the boys back up here and I'd like you to spend a few minutes with Nicky and help him."

"I don't need help," Nick protested. "I'm not a baby."

"I wasn't saying you were, buddy," Natalie reassured him. "I was just suggesting to Jake that he give us a hand before he takes off to flirt with girls. I'd hate to tell my mom that he left me all alone to clean up and I had to carry everything back to the cottage by myself, leaving you boys to wander along the highway." Her cold, hazel daggers fixed on Jake.

"Okay, stop." Jake raised his hand. "I'll help get all the bags picked up, and we'll all walk back to the cottage *together*. You'll have a chance to relax and get changed. I just want to head over to the diner for a few minutes."

"I know exactly what you want," She cracked. "You want to be the typical guy and show off your moves to that hot girl from Georgia." Her voice pitched loud enough for one of the nearby moms to glance over her People magazine and stare at Jake.

"Oh my gosh," Natalie taunted. "You are blushing. Oooh, I was right."

Jake replied in a hushed tone. "Okay, yes, I want to go and talk with the girls. I haven't seen Bonnie in a while and she is one of my few non-related friends out here. And, yes, her cousin is…pretty."

"I knew it." Natalie retorted.

They gathered the bags together as Matt and Brian came to shore.

Back at the cottage, the boys went upstairs to change while Natalie loaded the items from the fridge into the cooler.

"I'll see you in a few." Jake turned towards the door, trying not to miss his window.

"Just to make sure you aren't gone too long." Natalie stopped him and called upstairs, "Hey, Matty?"

"Yeah, Natalie?"

"Are you dressed?"

"Yeah, I'm ready to go." Matt came down the stairs with his bag.

"Would you be the coolest cousin in the whole world?"

"Of course, what do you need?"

"Jake here is going over to say bye to Mrs. Beck and Bonnie." She grabbed her purse. "Would you bring me back a super-cold Coca-Cola, please?"

"You betcha." Natalie handed him two bucks.

"And get something for yourself, too." She gave him her biggest smile.

Matt relished the fact that he was Natalie's favorite among the other cousins. "Thank you so much." Natalie winked at Jake. "You boys have fun."

"Yeah, thanks so much," Jake groaned as they left the

Chapter Nine

cottage.

"Okay, Matt." Jake got his attention as they neared the road. "Let's talk real quick."

"Yeah, Jake."

"Here are some quarters so you can play some of the video games, okay? I'm not gonna take too long, but I would appreciate having a few minutes with the girls. Do you follow me?"

"Oh, yeah, I gotcha, Jake. Just let me know when you're ready."

"Perfect." He gave Matt a thumbs up as they walked inside.

The diner was humming along with the lunchtime crowd. Leah and Bonnie were seated at a corner table by the jukebox.

The jukebox was the subject of some controversy within the Beck family. At least, between Mrs. Beck, her daughter, and her granddaughter, regarding what should be available for play. The standards such as "Achy Breaky Heart", "Baby, Baby", "Vogue", as well as Mariah Carey, Journey, Bryan Adams, and most Michael Jackson songs were allowed. Banned were songs like "I'm Too Sexy", "Never Gonna Get It", "Like a Virgin", and the artists Sir Mix-a-Lot, Guns N' Roses, and TLC. Along with anything that sounded *Alternative*. Mr. Beck and Bonnie's dad had a personal policy of not discussing the jukebox as no answer was ever the correct one for the women.

Bonnie was sipping her 7Up and poking a long, golden French fry in a sea of ketchup. Leah stared out the window at the cornfield that was swaying gently in the breeze, mirroring the turmoil in her heart. She sang along with Garth Brooks, almost as if she were in a place of her own. "I'll never reach my destination, if I never try, so I will sail my vessel 'til the river runs dry." She mouthed the words, blinking back a small tear as the song finished. Jake waved to Bonnie as he gave Matt a few more quarters.

Leah noticed him and regained her composure. "Do you always pay off your cousins so you can talk to girls?"

"Only the pretty ones," Jake brushed against Bonnie as

she blushed.

"So you do got it in you." Leah laughed out loud, easing up in her chair.

"Oh, that and then-some." Bonnie rolled her eyes at Jake as the song finished. "That's enough country." She put on "I'm Your Baby Tonight" and punched the numbers to add "Hold On" and "To Be With You" to the queue.

"There, that's more like it."

"I don't know. Farmer Tan seemed pretty happy singing along with Garth."

"That's all they listened to down in Cowboyland."

Jake was taken in by the southern girl seated across from him. Her long, flowing dark hair cascaded around her shoulders, a striking contrast to her eyes, a haunted-blue that seemed to hold a thousand secrets, set against her soft rounded face. Her lips curved into a smile that the Cheshire cat would view with jealousy.

"You gonna take a Polaroid or something?" Leah prodded back at Jake's obvious staring.

Caught looking, Jake covered with a topic shift. "So how do you like Wisconsin? Bet it's cool to be up here versus Georgia." His words fell flat and drew a look of disgust from Bonnie.

Leah got quiet for a second and stared back out to the fields. "It's alright. It's nice to get away from life for a minute."

"Oh." Jake looked at Bonnie, whose eyes had become searing laser beams. He chose to direct the conversation to her and caught up on how the school year had been. Of particular note, she mentioned that the guy she had been seeing was given a change-of-station to the Mediterranean.

Bonnie started to ask about Arizona when Matt walked up to the table and mentioned he was out of quarters. Jake looked back at Bonnie "It was good to catch up. Matt and I should get back to Natalie and the boys. Bonnie, I'll give you a call later, if that's cool?"

"That sounds good. You remember my second line?"

"Yup, 2BO-NNIE, never forgot it," he winked.

Chapter Nine

"Talk to you later."

"Have a good afternoon, ladies."

"You as well, Farmer Tan." The warmth in Leah's words was not lost on Jake, and the call he planned for later.

"Let's go, Matt, don't forget the soda."

"Already got it." Matt held up the bottle as they headed toward the door.

"Drive safe, Jake, and tell your Grandpa to come fishing next time. Harold would love to see him," Clara's voice came from behind the counter.

"I will, Mrs. Beck," he called back as they left the cool air conditioning into the June afternoon.

"Here's your Coke, Natalie." Matt handed the cold soda to her as they walked in the door.

"Thank you, Matty," she scrutinized Jake's cheery disposition. "And how was your time over there, Jake? Did you flirt with the pretty southern girl?"

"Shush, Natalie." Jake opened the fridge to hide his blush. "Thank you for getting everything packed up."

"No problem." She looked at the boys. "Alright, let's go."

Jake grabbed the remaining bags as they went to the car. Soon, the Buick was backing up and making its way up the rural route, headed back to the freeway. Natalie noticed Jake's quiet demeanor on the ride home and wondered what he was thinking as he stared out at the road ahead.

Chapter Ten
Eternal Flame

Leah sat on Bonnie's double bed in the upstairs bedroom as her cousin sorted through clothes in a basket on the desk. The TV played Murphy Brown in the background. Leah glanced at the bed sheets. "Still into New Kids on the Block?" She teased her cousin.

"Not like three years ago," Bonnie laughed. "As much hassle as mom went through to find them, I haven't had the heart to tell her I want something new."

"No opinion on the other brothers, but I saw the new Calvin Klein ad and Mark Wahlberg is pretty smoking hot." Leah gave a wry grin.

"I definitely agree with you there."

The tinny ring of the hot-pink cordless phone startled Bonnie. She glanced at the clock. "That could be Jake."

"May I answer?" Leah had a mischievous look on her face.

"Be nice and make sure it's him."

"I'm always nice." Leah reached the phone before the answering machine picked up and hit the speaker button.

"Hello?" A slow drawl greeted him.

"Leah? Is Bonnie there?"

"You're on speaker, Jake, I can hear you."

"What are you girls doing?"

"Reading Tiger Beat and talking about how hot Keanu Reeves and River Phoenix are," Bonnie swooned into the speaker.

"I mean, I think Keanu Reeves is amazing as an actor. Point Break was beyond awesome. And River Phoenix can pretty much play anything. He's hard to describe."

Chapter Ten

"Yeah, I would recommend *Dogfight*. I saw it a few times; it's an amazing film." Leah leaned over the phone. "And, *Bill and Ted's Excellent Adventure* has a lot more nuance than people give it credit for. But you have to really watch it to see the little things they bring out in it."

"Wow, I liked that one. It was pretty funny. You see a lot of movies?"

"Yeah, my friend Kyle's family is part of Carmike Cinemas. I worked with him and my ex-boyfriend, David, at the one of the theaters his dad manages."

"That's pretty cool, do you still work there? There are some awesome films coming out this summer."

"No, not since David and I broke up. It wasn't the same, working together afterwards. I still go there with my friends. Kyle hooks us up for premieres."

"Oh, I get that."

Bonnie jumped into the conversation she was feeling excluded from. "It's just a boring Monday night, Jake. Watching a Murphy Brown rerun. What are you doing?"

"Listening to the Brewers' game and flipping through my grandpa's stacks of Reader's Digests and National Geographics."

"National Geographics?" Leah teased. "Looking for pictures of tribal women?"

"What? No!" Jake blurted out.

Bonnie laughed. "Wow, that quick denial makes it sound like a yes!"

Jake started to stumble around to defend himself before Bonnie interrupted him, "Jeez, Jake, just messing with you."

"So, Farmer Tan, what are your plans for tomorrow?"

"I know we're taking the kids to lunch at George Webb's near the village, there is a waitress there she helps out. What's on your schedule?"

Bonnie glanced at her cousin, "I was thinking about taking Leah out to Mayfair Mall. I may get Funky Divas at Sam Goody, and Leah might want to get a new swimsuit at Wet Seal so she can actually catch some rays and improve her tan."

Jake was confused. "A better swimsuit?"

Eternal Flame

"Exactly, Farmer Tan. Dad would have me swimming in a suit from the nineteen-fifties if he could. I figured you'd understand this with all your sun-kissed days in the desert."

"Oh, yeah." Jake wistfully envisioned some ideas of a better swimsuit.

"Don't get too carried away with your imagination there, Mr. Footloose-and-Fancy-Free," Bonnie teased as her voice moved toward what she wondered in her heart. "But I was gonna ask, what happened back in Arizona? You wrote in your last letter that you broke up. I was kind of surprised. You dated for almost three years."

"The same trust issues I was struggling with last summer, they didn't go away, they just got worse. We started growing distant and she decided to see someone else."

"Yeah I know how that goes," Leah shook her head. "But if there were that many problems for so long, how did you guys ever start all the fireworks in the first place?"

Jake fidgeted with the magazine in his lap. "We knew each other when we were little, through fourth grade, until her family moved to Phoenix. Yet, on the first day of my freshman year, I saw her between classes. She had grown up, but those amber golden eyes were still the same as when we were kids..."

His voice trailed off for a moment, lost in memory. "She was having a horrible first day. She had gotten her classes mixed up, two girls hassled her for what she was wearing, and Senior guys had been crude, hitting on her. At lunch I crossed the courtyard. There she was, sitting alone, her face in her hands. I sat down beside her. 'Hey, Marty, I haven't seen you in forever! It's so good to see you. Mind if I join you?'

"She looked up at me, her eyes all red and puffy, 'Jacob, I can't believe it–I've missed you!' and she hugged me just like she did the day she moved, and that was it."

"Oh, I know." a chaffed resentment touched Bonnie's words. "You called me, which I'm surprised your mom didn't kill you over the long distance charges. You babbled like a fool for an hour before I got a word in."

"I invited her to be part of our group and we all hung

Chapter Ten

out," Jake continued. "The Perez family are a lot of fun and our parents got along as well. But Marta is Marta. She knows she's beautiful and because she's the only girl with her brothers, she is a total drama queen. Within a year, she rose in the social hierarchy at the high school. I wondered if I was good enough for her over the last year. Who she was three years ago and who she is today are completely different. It became all about prestige: who we were with, where we were, and, soon, she wasn't sure about my friends. Like Curtis and Susan. I mean, Curtis Ringo is about as country as you can get and Susan is a total computer nerd, which makes it weird they're dating, but that whole look didn't fit Marta's image anymore."

"Wait," Leah was suddenly interested. "Curtis Ringo? Is he related to the outlaw Johnny Ringo?"

Jake chuckled. "I guess he's somehow related to the guy from Tombstone. The Ringo's have been in Arizona a long time. Curtis definitely thinks he's a full-on cowboy. I've got a picture somewhere that makes him look like he just stepped off a trail drive."

"So, what's his girlfriend like? A total 'aww shucks' Annie Oakley?"

"No, not even close. Susan Serrano is as feisty as a badger and grade-curve-killer smart, but she loves her cowboy."

"So enough about your high-school yearbook, Jake," Leah was eager to get back to the gossip. "How'd you lose the Spanish princess?"

Jake hesitated. "Bonnie—"

"What?" Bonnie deflected. "She wasn't MY girlfriend."

"Because you know," Jake mumbled.

Leah glanced at the phone, then back at her cousin whose cheeks were shading crimson. "What do you know?"

A curdled sarcasm dripped from her voice. "The main problem was not listening to each other, ignoring their true feelings, and Jake putting his *needs* first. Am I right?"

"Whoa, hold on!" Jake protested. "That's not the whole story."

"Neither is what I said." Annoyance laced her voice. "I

mean, last summer you poured your heart out about how much you loved Marta, but you weren't sure if her feelings were as strong, all your insecurities swirling around as we sprawled out on the dock, watching the stars. Trust me, Jake, I remember."

Bonnie took a breath as her heart pulsed through her voice. "And I'll be honest, Jake. I've listened and listened to you for years now, but sometimes you need to listen, too. Just take a second to stop and pay more attention to what's actually there, not just what you're wishing for. Maybe then you wouldn't miss what's right in front of you."

Leah looked at her cousin, bewildered.

Jake remained silent until she finished. "What are you saying, Bonnie? I don't follow you."

"Of course you don't, Jake." Pain clipped her voice. "It's getting late. Have fun with your cousins tomorrow."

"Bonnie?! " Jake stammered. "The reason I called. I wondered if you wanted to grab lunch on Thursday? We can talk more then, okay?"

Silence.

"Night, Leah."

"Night, Farmer Tan." Leah answered softly as Bonnie hung up the call.

Her cheeks were flushed and anger was swimming in her eyes as she exhaled.

"Okay, cuz." Leah leaned back, her elbow on Donnie Wahlberg. "You gotta fill me in. What the heck was that all about?"

Bonnie didn't answer, but her eyes spoke for her.

"Oh my God, how long have you liked Jake?"

Bonnie stared out the window at the starry night. "Seems like forever, I guess. It probably started that first summer after fifth grade when he started coming up for two months each year. My grandma and his would meet up and we spent practically our entire summers together. It went on like that for four years. We were inseparable, the best of friends." Her voice was hollow as she sat, reliving those memories. "We actually kissed once."

"Shut up! No way!"

Chapter Ten

Still gazing out the window Bonnie continued. "It was the summer before freshman year, out on the boat dock. We sat and watched the sunset, holding hands. I poured my heart out to him, telling him how much he meant to me and that I'd always cared for him. You know, the whole middle-school romantic 'I've discovered poetry' phase. I think he was a little surprised by it, as he was silent for like five minutes, which is unusual for Jake, because he never shuts up. "Finally, he spoke, 'Bonnie, you're the closest friend I've ever had. You mean so much to me, and I love you, too.' And then we kissed. It was late July, near the end of his visit."

Bonnie stretched back on the bed, her face shared the emotions within her heart.

"We didn't talk much about it after that. There wasn't any discussion of being boyfriend and girlfriend or anything. I mean, he lived in Arizona and I lived in Wisconsin. We wrote letters that August. But I'll never forget that afternoon sitting in my room, looking over my first week's Algebra homework, when he called my line. He babbled on and on about this girl he'd grown up with who was back at school, how crazy it was, and how much he'd missed her. It hit me so hard, I muted the phone as I cried."

Leah slipped her hand across to Bonnie's as she worked through her heart's reality.

"I care about Jake so much and when Marta treated him like crap over the last year, I almost didn't want to hear about it because it hurts me to see him go through it. I wanted so badly to say, 'I told you so.' All he talked about were the problems Marta caused, how she didn't trust him, and even got jealous of pictures with me. It tore me up. Because all this time I still loved him. She hugged her cousin tightly. Bonnie caught her breath and wiped her eyes as she looked at Leah with a face of resignation. "And now I feel invisible all over again."

"What are you talking about?" Leah stood, her hand on her hip.

Bonnie was too tired to argue. "If you can't see it, I'll leave your blinders where they are." She turned off the TV and headed toward the bathroom.

"Well, good night." Leah headed downstairs to the guest room, her mind at a loss for her cousin's reaction.

Chapter Eleven
Step by Step

"Swear to God, Brian, if you push Nick in the river, I'll beat your ass and tell Mom!" Natalie's voice rang out from behind Jake as he strolled along the river trail.

"I wasn't pushing, just messing around," Brian hollered back.

"Nu-uh, you said you were gonna throw me in," Nick whined.

"Stop tattling, Nick," Matt pleaded, trying to calm his brother and cool down their cousin.

"I wasn't tattling! Brian said he was—" Nick sputtered as Jake turned around.

"Alright, I don't care who started it, but knock it off or there'll be trouble for all of you. Understood?" Jake looked the boys firmly in the eye.

A mumbled, "Yes, Jake" came from the three before Nick started in again about how it wasn't his fault.

Natalie had had enough.

"Nicky, why don't you walk with me for a minute?"

Natalie and Nick set off at a leisurely pace, heading towards the playground.

The older boys raced ahead across the vast green spaces bordering the river. Natalie kept a watchful eye, calling out for them to stay away from the water. The numerous shallow areas and gravel eddies offered breaks between the dense bushes and trees lining the shore. Jake decided to have some fun showing the boys the hidden treasures along the riverbank.

Deciding to give them a little leeway, much to Natalie's dismay, Jake and the two boys were soon barefoot and waded in a large pool in search of crayfish. Matt found two and came up the grass to show Natalie, who feigned excitement for her cousin, but kept her distance.

Natalie went on ahead of them, allowing Nick to play at the various playgrounds along the parkway. It was a quarter-to-one when they reached the village. The restaurant, George Webb's, was located near the old brick buildings that marked the village's founding one hundred and fifty years before. It's simple and classic style kept it one of Lucy's favorites over the years.

The restaurant was buzzing with the lunch crowd. Julie saw them and, after a few minutes, had a table ready for the group. Julie took down their drink orders and told Natalie she would be back when Lucy came in.

Gram arrived just as her unsweetened tea with two lemons was delivered to her spot at the table. Chicken nuggets and burgers were the boys' choices for the day. Natalie opted for a grilled chicken sandwich, while Lucy ordered a BLT with a side salad. Jake decided on a third-pound burger with all the toppings (minus onions).

As they waited for their orders, Lucy inquired about the morning's events. The boys, in a rapid-fire exchange, recounted their adventures.

She asked Jake about his plans for Wednesday, as he'd requested the car. Natalie jumped into the conversation, "It's cuz he wants to flirt with Bonnie's pretty cousin," she shouted.

Jake blushed as Gram, with her firm and enunciated voice, reminded Natalie to lower hers, as they were in a restaurant. The entrees arrived and the conversation was lost in passing food and intermittent requests for ketchup or salt.

When the plates were mostly cleared, Lucy looked to her eldest grandchild, "Jake, if you want to spend the day in Waukesha, visiting Bonnie, I don't see a problem with that. Just be back by a decent hour and make sure there's gas in the car."

"Yes, Gram."

"Okay, then that's settled. Natalie, would you help me get the boys out to the car?" As Natalie readily agreed, Gram turned back to Jake. "Please pay the bill and leave a rest for Julie. She's got a lot of mouths to feed." She handed him a hundred-dollar

Chapter Eleven

bill and walked out to the car.

    That evening, Jake relaxed on the living room couch with a Reader's Digest condensed novel of Tom Clancy's *Patriot Games* while his grandparents were watching Cheers on the TV. Though, "watching" would be an overstatement. Alvin leaned back on the couch, engrossed in his latest crossword puzzle, while Lucy read notes from the last city-council meeting. She was accompanied by the ruffled snoring of a pug curled up with her on the Lay-z-boy.

    "I tell you, Alvin, I'm not sure about people these days. No sense of common decency," She fumed.

    "I'm sure you'll let them know, Lucy," Alvin replied without looking up. "Getting ready for Thursday?"

    "Yes, and don't you worry, I'll be front and center. Ross better be ready."

    "I'm sure he can't wait," He muttered, making a mental note to avoid Ross at the Bluemound Bowl.

    The clattering of the phone broke the lull in conversation. Gram reached for the phone. "Oh, Hi Bonnie. Jake? Sure, hang on." She smiled toward her grandson.

    "I'll take it upstairs. Night, Gram. Night, Grandpa."

    "Night, Jake. Let me know when you're on."

    "Thanks, Gram." Jake headed upstairs and picked up the cordless from the end table, confirming to his grandma that he had it.

    "Bye, Bonnie. Tell Betty I said 'hi', dear."

    "I will," Bonnie replied as she and Jake heard the other line click.

    Jake settled back on the couch. "Hey, Bonnie, what are you up to?"

    "Just some wild girl stuff," she teased. "Painting nails, listening to Nirvana – you know, the usual."

    "Really? Cool," Jake replied.

    "Leah is reading some trashy romance novel. I'm trying to watch 90210."

    "Hi, Farmer Tan! And FYI, it's *Outlander* – high

literature," Leah chimed in playfully.
"So, Jake, you still got wheels for tomorrow?"
"Yeah. Did you still want to meet up for breakfast?"
Bonnie thought for a second. "Yes, we were thinking about 10:30. That way, we have time and no rush before the lunch crowd gets in."
"Hopefully we can find a place to park."
"Don't forget your quarters. Dave's Restaurant is right on the main drag," Bonnie reminded him
"I know, I look forward to catching up with you without my cousins running a timer."
"That will be nice. And Dave's has the best pancakes in town. If you want, we can walk around after."
"We should have time. So, Leah, did you find anything at Mayfair?"
"And why would you be curious about that, Farmer Tan?"
"I don't know." Jake fished a little more, "You mentioned 'shopping' for something today."
"Did we, now?" Bonnie snapped as she leaned toward the phone. "And since when have you *ever* been interested in shopping?"
"I think Jake wants to know what I got." A flirtatiousness filled Leah's voice, prodding Bonnie's temper as she listened. "And for your information, Mr. Nosey, I'm not going to tell you. You will just have to wait and see."
"Oh, so…when will I get to see it?" Jake's rapt interest was a bit too much for Bonnie's liking.
"Oh my gosh. Seriously, is that all you think about? Wow!"
Jake backtracked to not sound like a creep. "You all did say you were gonna look for a—"
"A swimsuit, Jake," Bonnie's voice rising. "A swimsuit. Were you hoping for some wild bikini fashion show? Cause, seriously, this is for my grandparent's beach. Like that would fly in any century."
Her words got ahead of her breath. "Yes, *we* did find

Chapter Eleven

suits, I got one too, so you know, and if you are able to control yourself, you might get to see it." With her lecture finished she lowered her tone and stepped off her verbal soapbox. Leah mouthed, "What was that?" at her cousin, as Bonnie tried to cool down.

Jake tried to stay out of the line of fire, "Oh, I'm glad you found one. So Leah, do you like what you picked out?"

"Yes, Jake, it's quite nice and comfortable, actually. And it's a pretty lime green."

"Cool. I think I'm going back to the lake on Friday with Grandpa."

"Really?" Bonnie feigned surprise. "You all were just there Monday."

"Thursday night is some meeting at the high school that Grams is going ballistic over and Grandpa doesn't want to be in town the day after."

"That definitely sounds like your gram. So what is it this time?"

"I have no idea, and I'm not sure I want to ask."

"We are gonna be at the lake Friday, Leah, remember?" Bonnie looked toward her cousin.

"Oh, that's right, our shift at the diner."

"But only until early afternoon. We can probably go swimming after, if you all are done fishing."

"I'm assuming your grandfather will be joining me and my grandpa." Jake's thoughts drifted to getting a chance to fish for once.

"I'm sure he will, he never misses a chance to go fishing."

A yawn snuck into Bonnie's voice as she looked at the clock, "I'm thinking we are gonna start getting ready for bed."

"I'm already pretty comfortable and ready for bed, just waiting for my company to join me."

"Really, who might that be?" Leah wondered aloud.

"I'll let her say hello." Jake scooped up the dog that was snuffling around the room and laid her on the fluffy comforter.

"Hi, Maggie," Bonnie called to the dog.

Maggie gave her standard reply into the phone.

Step by Step

"Aww, she sounds adorable," Leah laid her head alongside the phone

"That makes two," Jake teased into the phone as the dog burrowed into the covers.

Bonnie glared at Leah, grabbing her robe off the door hook.

"You and your snuggle-buddy get some sleep and I'll see you in the morning." Leah purred back

"Sounds good. Sweet dreams, Leah. Goodnight."

"Goodnight, Farmer Tan," Leah let her words drift through the phone. "Sweet dreams."

Jake hung up the receiver, her voice carrying him off to sleep.

Leah heard the bathroom door slam as the call ended.

Chapter Twelve
Tom's Diner

Jake woke up and rummaged through his suitcase until he found his Nirvana t-shirt. The jeans he grabbed had seen better days but, like his Pyros, they fit like an old friend. He swung around the bottom banister, almost colliding with Gram, who was carrying a basket, piled high with laundry.

"Careful, boy." She teetered for a moment to not spill the basket and Jacob helped her place it on an end table. "You seem in good spirits today."

"It's going to be an awesome day."

"What time do you plan on heading out this morning?"

"Ten o'clock."

"It's still early. Your grandpa's out on the back porch, probably complaining about the squirrels. You should go grab a cup of coffee with him. I think you two need to chat."

"I know I need to figure out the summer plans." Jake poured himself a cup of Maxwell House from the coffee pot and grabbed some breakfast before he headed to the porch.

"Morning, Grandpa," Jake said, taking a seat. He placed the mug and bowl of Basic 4 on the coffee table.

"Morning, Jake." A bit of the sun shone upon the old man's jaw. "Beautiful day out."

"It sure is. Gram mentioned you wanted to talk with me."

"I did." Alvin took a sip of his coffee. "Now, I'm glad you're up here for the summer to help with the cottage. And I'm fine with you staying by yourself as you're almost eighteen. But I have a favor to ask."

"Sure, of course."

"Figured that'd be your answer. Since you'll be out there, I'm going to let you take the Cutlass. That way, I won't

Tom's Diner

have to tie up a car, and your grandmother is rather fond of her Mercury."

"Does that old car still run?" Jake raised an eyebrow.

"It does," Alvin nodded. "I had it in the shop this spring and that 442 is running fine. It just needs a little attention from time to time. You'll have to learn to not over-push it – kind of like your grandma," he chuckled.

Jake spit his coffee. "I gotcha, Grandpa."

"Now, here's the other part of the deal. I'm not worried about you trashing the place or throwing wild parties–your Aunt would tack your hide to the wall for that–but I do want you to do one thing for me. Every Thursday, I want you to spend the day with your Great-Aunt Edith."

"Okay," Jake shrugged. "I'm fine with that. I like Aunt Edith. I think she likes me, too."

"Jake, that's a worry you won't have with Edith," he rolled his eyes. "In all her life, speaking her mind has never been an issue–ever."

Jake was quite familiar with his aunt's sharp tongue, "I'll head over tomorrow. What time?"

"She'll be expecting you around quarter-to-ten." Alvin gave him a firm look. "Be on time."

"I will be," Jake promised.

"Be careful; she's almost ninety-five. She can't see super well and she will need extra time, but her mind is sharp as a tack," warned Alvin.

"You got it, Grandpa."

"Wonderful," Alvin clasped his hands. "Your grandmother and Aunt will be quite pleased with you helping. And I'll see if I can get the women to let you stay out at the lake starting this weekend. But I need to see real work done or this will end."

"It will be. Is Uncle Ron going to come out, also? I know I'll need help with the roof."

"Don't worry about that, there will be a few workdays on the weekends where we'll have a bunch of people out. I'll see if I can get one set for this Saturday or Sunday afternoon. That

Chapter Twelve

way, your Aunt Evelyn can give you a rundown of everything at the cottage and some specifics about staying there. She has a list or two waiting for you, I guarantee it." He grinned at Jake.

"Oh, I am sure."

"Perfect. I hope you have a nice day with Bonnie and her cousin,"

"Thanks, Grandpa. I'll see you later."

Jake headed inside, toward the staircase. Lucy turned off the Hoover vacuum in the living room when she saw him.

"You boys talk?"

"Yes, I'm spending tomorrow with Aunt Edith."

"Good," she smiled to herself. "Now remember to drive safely. I hope you enjoy your time with Bonnie and her cousin. But please don't stay out too late. Traffic gets bad on the expressway and you're still learning to drive, in my opinion. The Cutlass keys are on the hook for you."

"Yes, Gram. I'm going to go upstairs to get ready before I leave."

"Get ready?" Gram arched her brow. "You look dressed to me."

"I just want to clean up a little." He ran a hand over his chin." I could probably use a shave."

"Hmm, never seen you worry about that before," Gram caught his eye. "Jake, just remember, ribbons and bows only hide what's inside."

"I know," he assured her as he went upstairs to finish getting ready.

Jake knew the way to Waukesha like the back of his hand. He always enjoyed watching the landscape slowly shift. But what used to be endless fields was turning into houses, strip malls, and parking lots. Yet, through it all, Dave's Restaurant on Main Street was still dishing out breakfast and burgers like it had since the fifties.

Jake found a spot near the restaurant, dropped two quarters in the parking meter, and made his way inside. The diner was quiet, just a few regulars nursing their coffees at the counter. Knowing Bonnie's habit of running late, he asked for a

Tom's Diner

corner booth and ordered his coffee, one cream with no sugar, a 7 Up for Bonnie, and took a guess at sweet tea for Leah.

It was twenty minutes before the girls came through the door, laughing. Bonnie wore her go-to summer outfit of jean shorts and a floral shirt, brown curls spilling out under her cream beret. Leah sported an Adidas t-shirt and a tennis skirt, looking ready to take the court. Her hair flowed loose around bright-yellow sunglasses.

"Morning, Farmer Tan," Leah drawled.

Bonnie sipped her soda. "Thanks for ordering drinks."

"Yes, thank you," echoed Leah. "What are you thinking about for breakfast?"

Jake glanced at his menu again. "Probably a ham-and-cheese omelet with rye toast."

"I'm getting the blueberry pancakes special," Bonnie pointed to the card on the napkin holder.

Leah looked over the menu at Jake. "I'd love some eggs, but I also love French toast. Want to share? I've discovered there isn't a place north of Tennessee that understands how to make grits properly."

"Sounds good to me," Jake nodded as they placed their orders.

"So, how's your trip so far?" Bonnie asked Jake.

"Not bad," he replied. "Tomorrow I'm spending the day with Aunt Edith and I'm starting to plan a few things, like maybe a Cubs game with Uncle Bobby and catch a show at Summerfest."

"I'd like to see a Cubs game," Bonnie moved her chair closer to Jake.

"What's Summerfest?" Leah inquired.

"It's a huge multi-day music festival," Jake explained. "All types of music."

"We can take a look," Bonnie spotted an abandoned Sentinel paper at a nearby table. She returned with the paper as it was divided between them. Leah grabbing the sports section, Bonnie the entertainment pages, and Jake the comics.

"Wow." Bonnie looked through a Summerfest Ad. "There

Chapter Twelve

are some bomb acts each night. Metallica, John Mellancamp, Chicago, Paula Abdul, and Michael Bolton."

"I love Michael Bolton." Leah's eyes lit up.

"Oh, snap, here we go." Bonnie looked at the ceiling.

"No way, so do I." Jake put down the comics. "Which song is your favorite?"

"Before you both profess your undying love for a man with longer hair than mine, please know there are other bands that will be there." Bonnie cringed.

"But they're not Michael Bolton." Leah stuck out her tongue.

Bonnie's high-stack of blueberry pancakes and blueberry syrup were delivered and Leah asked for an extra plate. The smell of cinnamon filled the air as the waitress returned with their meals and Jake and Leah began splitting the omelet and French toast.

The table was quiet as they enjoyed the comfort food, other than requests for condiments.

Jake got a refill on he coffee and turned to Leah with a hopeful smile. "Well, Leah, now that we have a few minutes, you seemed to have a question the other night that was left unasked. Just curious, what was it?"

Bonnie watched a flicker of something cross Leah's face – a hint of amusement, maybe even a challenge. Leah gave a side glance at her cousin as she leaned forward, locking into a gaze with Jake that sent a jolt through Bonnie.

"Yes, I do have a question for you, Farmer Tan. Why are you spending your summers out here when you could be home, chasing hot Cali girls?"

The question hung heavy in the air and Bonnie felt a familiar pang that she couldn't describe. It was a question she'd probably asked herself a hundred times. She forced a smile, trying to appear unfazed, but deep down, she longed to hear Jake's answer–longed for something that might hint at the connection her heart longed to be there.

Jake attempted bad origami with his napkin and he weighed his answer. "I can't remember the first few summers we

Tom's Diner

came here, I was so young. Over the years, things steadily got worse at home." Jake pondered how much he wanted to share. "By the time I was in fifth grade, Mom was not doing well. And Dad had to travel, so we came here. I'm sure you remember."

"I remember." Bonnie let her mind wander to hose days. "Your Aunt Evelyn set it up so Kyle could go to summer camp with your cousin and you were driving your grandfather crazy. So I've heard."

"Gram and Grandpa were still working a lot in the office with Uncle Emmit and so one morning we came out early to the farm. There, sitting on a feed bag, was a girl in overalls with long curly brown hair talking to a chicken like it was the most intriguing conversation she'd ever had."

"Really? Talking to a chicken?" Leah glanced at Bonnie, who turned red.

"In my defense, Gertrude was quite the conversationalist," Bonnie muttered.

"And that was the start of endless days we spent exploring every inch of that farm, woods, and the lake."

"Just you and I," Bonnie added to the memory. "Swimming, fishing, and nearly drowning trying to sail the Sunfish."

"Hey, we figured it out pretty quick, as long as there was wind."

"Or begging someone to tow us back when we lost it," Bonnie laughed, but the laughter felt hollow.

"Those were good times, just us. Remember, Bonnie?"

Bonnie offered a small, sad curve to her lips, as something flickered deeper in her eyes. "Those were the days. Sometimes I wish I could freeze time in a bottle and keep them forever." Her voice was quiet, the words heavy with a longing she couldn't quite hide.

"Me too," Jake admitted. "You've always been one of my closest friends. Those summers, we lived them to the max. All the way up until that last one after—"

"Eighth grade," Bonnie whispered. "That summer, when you stayed after your parents and Kyle left. Three weeks, just

Chapter Twelve

you and me." The memory of their twilight kiss hung between them, unspoken but there. It was the summer she realized the truth about her own heart–the love she'd felt for him that he never returned.

"Yeah," said Jake, his voice tight, a knot of unresolved emotions wrestled in his chest.

He let out a breath, "After that, we stopped coming up for the whole summer. Baseball leagues, camps. Things changed. This year, I wanted something different. This is probably my last summer where I can just be up here and have fun. Next summer, I don't know. I might head out early to Ohio and start getting ready for college."

"So you really are skipping Stanford?" Bonnie tried to move words past the pain in her heart.

Jake tried to keep his voice light, but it cracked. "It's going to cost me, but it's my choice."

"That's a big decision."

"Wow, Stanford," Leah was surprised. "Your parents would pay for you to go there?"

"Yes, and this moron is turning it down," Bonnie shook her head.

"Of all places, why Ohio?" Leah's curiosity was clear.

"We have some family in Ohio," Jake explained between bites of his French toast. "Plus, I'd actually like to experience all four seasons for a change."

"Let me tell you, Jake. That winter season you're longing for? Trust me, it's highly overrated. The snow gets old fast." Bonnie's tone was as cold as a frosty morning.

"Bobby says Ohio isn't as bad as long as you aren't near the lake," Jake turned in his chair. "How about you, Leah? What's your story?"

Bonnie tried to interject, "Leah, you don't—"

Leah cut her off. "It's okay, Bonnie. It's a fair question. But, Jake, it's not something I want to talk about in a diner."

Jake saw there was a lot more to this than he realized. "When you're ready, I'd love to hear it."

Then it happened. Leah reached out for a napkin, her

Tom's Diner

hand brushing against Jake's. Their eyes meeting, and in that brief moment, Bonnie saw it–the spark of connection igniting between them. It was subtle, but undeniable, a flicker of something that could grow into more.

Lost in the moment, Leah caught herself, "I'd like that." Her eyes fixed on him.

A bitter ache settled deep in Bonnie's chest, the sting of watching Leah find something she'd long dreamed of having.

Pushing through her emotions, she forced her voice lighter than it felt, "What's the plan for today, Jake?" She poked at his shoulder.

"Nothing really, what are yours for the afternoon?" Jake inquired.

"Well, mine got changed. I need to head back home and get a list my mom put together for Woodman's," Bonnie replied. "And that will probably take the afternoon."

"Woodman's? I love Woodman's. I could go with you guys, I would just need to stop by to see if Gram needs anything."

"What's Woodman's?" Leah was confused.

"It's the big farmer's co-op store," Bonnie motioned the size with her hands. "They just opened it in Kenosha like two years ago. It's—"

"Wait," interrupted Leah. "You guys are getting all worked up over a grocery store?"

"Woodman's is not just any grocery store, it's like the king of grocery stores," Bonnie answered with an indignant tone.

Leah looked humored. "You both need to get out more."

"You wait. My dad said this one is the largest grocery store in the country."

"I guess that sounds a little interesting. You coming along, Farmer Tan?"

"Yes, If you can pick me up at Gram's on your way down."

After finishing their breakfast, Jake paid for the meal while Bonnie covered the tip. Bonnie headed home and soon was stopping by the Stanton house to pick up Jake.

Chapter Twelve

"Okay, I have to admit, that was not your regular grocery store," said Leah as she helped Bonnie and Jake unload the overflowing cart into the car.

"We told you," grinned Bonnie.

"Mhmm," said Jake with his mouth full of brick cheese curds. "These alone are worth the drive."

"I swear, I thought, between you two, we'd need to call for a second car with all the stuff you guys bought," laughed Leah.

"We don't come down often," said Bonnie. "Mom has a list on the fridge that she just adds to until it's long enough to go and we stock up. Grandma Beck likes to have certain types of cheese for the diner."

"And the honeycomb for my grandma and her allergies and, of course, grandpa's stinky cheese," said Jake, crinkling his nose.

"Dear God, please make sure that is sealed before we close the windows," Leah was still feeling nauseated from when Jake shoved it in her face. "Do people really eat that?"

"My grandfather would eat it every day if he could," laughed Jake.

"Your poor Grandma."

Jake waved bye, setting his bags on the porch as Bonnie pulled away, the car still full of groceries. Silence filled the air as Bonnie's heart and mind were engulfed with emotion.

Bonnie gripped the steering wheel tight, the words starting before she could stop them. "I've never understood that about you," she mumbled, glancing over at Leah.

Leah arched a brow, already having a pretty good idea. "Understood what?"

"You always get the guy, Leah. You just… bat your eyes, lay on that accent, and they're hooked."

Leah's eyes sparkled with a playful grin. "Woah, cuz. Back that up. What exactly are you accusing me of?"

Bonnie shot her a sidelong glare. "Accusing? Stating facts isn't accusing."

Leah leaned back, crossing her arms. "Alright, then.

"What are these 'facts'?"

Bonnie hesitated, but the words were already there. "I care so much for Jake. You *know* that, Leah. But you flirt with him until his head's spinning."

Leah gave a defensive shrug. "So I flirt a little. You need to chill. I'm not trying to put your fire out."

The response cut deep. Across the front seat, Leah could feel Bonnie's simmering frustration.

They drove in silence for some time before Leah spoke. "Here's the bigger issue, Bonnie. You're there for him, you listen to him, but you don't actually *tell* him how you feel. And you never *ask* him."

"I do tell him."

"No, you don't. You talk to him like he's a kid. If you'd be a little more open and honest, maybe you'd actually get somewhere. My grandma always says men might 'hear' you, but they *listen* when you add a little honey to it."

Bonnie spit her words. "Honey, huh? I'd probably need to hit Jake over the head with a beehive to get his attention."

Bonnie's heart twisted, but she stayed quiet. Leah was always able to brush things off, to laugh and move on with guy stuff it seemed, while Bonnie just couldn't.

Leah broke the silence as they turned off the interstate. "Look, I've only got four more weeks here before my world gets flipped, cuz. I'm gonna keep being me, and you can be you. Deal?"

Bonnie swallowed, unsure if she could handle four more weeks of watching Jake's attention turn toward Leah's effortless charm. She gave a curt nod, though everything in her wanted to tell Leah she was tired of 'dealing' with it.

But as the silence stretched on, Bonnie realized Leah was already back to her usual self— like nothing had even been said. And somehow, that stung most of all.

Chapter Thirteen
November Rain

"Mom?" Bonnie came downstairs as Betty sorted through jars of jam, dividing the ones bound for the diner from those to keep at home.

"Yes?" Betty glanced up from her list at her daughter. The ashen look on Bonnie's face raised her radar. "What's the matter?"

"Nothing. I forgot something at the Stantons' place. I know Leah is staying in tonight, so I was gonna head back to the city," Bonnie carefully nuanced each word in her planned speech.

"Okay," Betty replied, knowing her daughter well enough to sense there were things left unsaid. "When do you think you'll be back? It's almost six-thirty."

"I don't know; it won't be super late, but it's summer," Bonnie put on her best 'Please, Mom' face.

"Call me if it's going to be after eleven-thirty."

"I will," Bonnie gave her mom a quick kiss and hurried out the door.

Bonnie pulled up to the Stanton house just shy of seven. She took her time walking up the flat stones that served as a makeshift path to the door before knocking on the large wood door.

"I'll get it, Grandpa," she heard Jake's voice and footsteps as he walked through the foyer. The door creaked open slowly, and Jake peered out, a puzzled look on his face. "Bonnie, what are you doing here?"

"Come on in, Bonnie," Lucy called from the living room.

"I won't be long, Mrs. Stanton," Bonnie replied. Then, lowered her voice and looked deep into his eyes. "You forgot something today."

Jake stared back at her dusty freckles as his mind flipped through its mental rolodex, coming up blank. "What did I forget?"

The response seared her soul. *Me,* was the word that screamed from her heart but not her lips. Keeping her plan on track, she began, "We had talked about catching a movie since I don't have to work much tomorrow, and you don't have to be at Edith's till mid-morning."

"Yeah, we did." Though he couldn't recall this, the urgency in her eyes hinted he should. "Grandma, I'm gonna head out with Bonnie for a while."

"Have a lovely time, dear," Lucy called back from the living room.

Jake glanced toward Bonnie's car parked on the street, checking if anyone else was in it. "So is..."

Bonnie saw his wandering eye and shut that door before he could open it. "Leah's taking a chill night." The words were a half-truth but sufficed. She had told her cousin to chill and that she was seeing Jake for the night. "You want to drive? The Oldsmobile is less cramped than my little car."

"What do you want to see?" Jake asked, reaching behind him for the keys on the metal windmill mail rack.

"*Far and Away* is starting at eight-thirty at the 41 Twin Drive-In." Bonnie reached for his hand, leading him down the steps.

"Gosh, I haven't been out there since Grandpa took us all to see *The Little Mermaid*," he reminisced, remembering a wild night, crammed into the station wagon with all his cousins.

"So, have you seen it?" Bonnie's eyes searched his.

"No, Allen took Laura to see it. He said it's shot in seventy millimeter, so it should be amazing on the drive-in screen. Have you?"

"I've been waiting," was all Jake heard when the 442 engine rumbled to life, missing the words, "for you."

Driving south, they passed the zoo and Bonnie mentioned the new Apes of Africa exhibit, where gorillas roamed in a more

Chapter Thirteen

natural habitat. Jake couldn't resist teasing Bonnie about her past obsession with petting a possum.

"I did get to," she reminded him, recalling her triumphant day in seventh grade and the photo of her with the zookeeper and possum that was still hanging on the wall, the little creature giving a wishful look that its press time would be over.

"After you convinced my Aunt Evelyn to ask for you. That was so embarrassing," Jake cringed at his aunt's persistence that got the photoshoot.

"I knew she'd make it happen." Bonnie thought warmly of her strategic actions that landed her that chance, proving to her brother that possums were cute, not scary.

Near the Franklin exit, Jake saw the McDonald's sign. "You hungry?"

"Maybe a little. What are you thinking?"

"I saw an ad for the Gold Medal Meal. The Dream Team cups are out and I want a Michael Jordan."

"No one has the Michael Jordan but, seriously, the triple burger? You're gonna have a heart attack at eighteen."

"At least I'll enjoy my heart attack," Jake joked, thumping his chest. "What do you want? And please, don't say a salad."

"A Big Mac and an apple pie, please, with a Sprite."

With their food ordered, they parked in a Kohl's grocery lot, where Jake devoured his triple burger to Bonnie's disgust. His fries and ketchup were spread out on the dash like a personal buffet. "Want any?" he offered.

"Nah, I'll save room for popcorn and Mike & Ikes at the movies."

Jake gagged, "I know they're your favorite, but all they do is stick to your teeth. They're so sugary and sweet."

"I know–that's why I love them."

"You would," Jake's voice was muffled with a mouth half-full of burger. Bonnie looked past him at the city skyline. It was the beginning of a beautiful evening.

Dinner finished, they got in line with the other cars on 241 for the drive-in and found a spot in the outer third row as the sun set. At the concession stand, they picked up popcorn, Mike

& Ikes for her, and Reese's Pieces and Twizzlers for Jake.

Dusk settled around them, and Bonnie placed her candy on the dash, the popcorn to her right. She shifted on the bench seat, glancing at Jake, whose eyes were fixed on the screen as the first trailer for a new Steven Seagal movie exploded onto the screen. His features seemed to stand out in the dim light: the strong jawline, the mess of brown hair, and those eyes she'd seen in so many dreams. He was so close, yet his heart felt like a satellite circling above—always in her orbit but out of reach.

Gathering her jean skort, Bonnie moved closer to him. Jake was oblivious as Elvis music filled the car and Nicholas Cage shouted into a payphone on the screen for the *Honeymoon in Vegas* trailer. His left hand rested on the driver door windowsill, reaching up for a french fry when he felt her knee brush against his in the footwell.

Noticing her leg joining his, he shifted to adjust his headrest, she seized the moment, sliding closer, leaning against his shoulder. Her eyes met his, and he strained his metal capacity to understand what was going on in her mind.

"Here comes your beehive," she thought, hoping he'd take the neon framed hint.

Bonnie snuggled against him as he adjusted the headrest, his mind caught between the emotions of the day and that moment.

He looked down into her soft eyes, which looked back at him with an emotion that wrestled with his soul. He felt so much for her and, in years past, had been so deeply connected to her. Hearing her talk about the struggles of fitting in with the other girls and her fears that she wasn't pretty enough or skinny enough or whatever other impossible bar she claimed she fell short of–Jake was always her encourager and defender, standing up for her when the barbs cut too sharply, and holding her close later when her heart would break. It stung, thinking about the frustration he felt in his recent breakup: the beautiful vulnerability he shared with Bonnie was a locked door with Marta. Yet, peering now into the open window of her soul, he felt fear. Fear that, somehow, he would hurt one of the most

Chapter Thirteen

beautiful flowers that had ever bloomed within his life. He felt a burning attraction to Leah but Bonnie was a strand woven deeply into the threads of his own life, a bond he would never betray.

He slid his arm around her, pulling her close as the car lights dimmed.

Bonnie wrapped her arm in his, and felt his fingers extend while his chest shuddered, a gesture she recognized since sixth grade–his struggle of what to do. She clasped his right hand, and they held each other in silence as the sweeping landscapes of Ireland filled the screen.

In that moment, Jake forgot about Marta, Leah, his parents, and left the worries of the world behind. It was just him and Bonnie, sharing time and space as they always had.

Bonnie found herself struggling through the movie *Far and Away*, seeing herself in Shannon and feeling that same love for Joseph. She gripped Jake's hand tight during the scene when Tom Cruise flirted with Grace, the burlesque girl, triggering Shannon's jealousy. Her thoughts drifted to the earlier bout with her cousin.

"You know they're married," she whispered.

"Who?" he asked.

"Tom Cruise and Nicole Kidman."

Jake nodded, releasing her hand and running it along her shoulder. She seemed to have a chill as the scene showed Shannon and Joseph braving a Boston winter, seeking shelter in a home they broke into for food.

During the tender scene in the dark, where Shannon asks Joseph to sit with her at the dinner table to pretend they are husband and wife, Bonnie slipped her hand behind his back and took his right hand tightly into hers, pulling it to her.

"Did you ever wonder what that land you dreamed of would look like?"

The line on the screen stirred them, away from the movie, and to a moonless night three years earlier.

"What do you think this is gonna be like in 20 years?" Bonnie had asked Jake.

"I hope I'll be here, with my wife and kids, sharing all

that we've found here," Jake had told her that night. "What do you think?"

"I can't imagine a dream any better," Bonnie had prayed to the stars above.

"I still have that dream." Bonnie squeezed Jake's hand, bringing them back to the present as she lifted her face to look into his. "Do you?"

The lack of words spoke more than any he could have said. The rejection crashing into the pain, as the waters straining in both their hearts released.

"Take me home," was all she found the breath to say as he held her.

"Bonnie."

"Jake, you've said enough; just take me home." She pulled away and looked out the window, shielding him from the view of her hurt.

Silence screamed louder than the static of the radio as Jake channel-surfed on the drive home.

Rolling up the gravel drive at the Stanton house, Bonnie finally found the strength to look at Jake.

"Why do you keep coming back?"

"What are you talking about?"

"Leah asked this morning why, year after year, even now when you could have traveled anywhere in this world, you came back here. Why?"

His soul spoke for him. "Because here I feel I'm home, with you."

Bonnie's face crumpled as she opened the door, hurrying to her car before Jake could hear her sobs.

Bonnie pulled up to the house, the lone light on in the living room. Her mom was up reading, waiting. Or worse, it was Leah. Her heart sank deeper as she wiped her bloodshot eyes and blew her nose before quietly walking up the steps and slipping the key in the lock, hoping that the light was on by accident. She stepped across the threshold, mentally counting the steps to the stairs and dreaming of being home free in her bed.

The flick of the lamp by the chair cast the shadow of her

Chapter Thirteen

mom.

"You okay?"

"Fine."

"What's wrong, Bee? Slow down." Betty moved to cross her path before she dashed like a scared rabbit up the stairs.

"Jake doesn't..." was all she could say.

Betty caught her as she collapsed into her, barely holding her from falling to the floor.

"Jake what?" Betty asked urgently, trying to decipher what had happened.

"Doesn't want me."

"What?" Betty knew that was nonsense. "What are you talking about? That boy would move the earth for you."

"He would." Bonnie's tears returned in a torrent. "Jake would do anything in the world for me, Mom. That's why I love him so much. He would move anything. But..." She held her mother's gaze. "But the door of his heart..."

As she laid on her bed that night, staring into the darkness, she thought of all the dreams that now evaporated into the void of a broken heart.

Chapter Fourteen
Born and Raised in Black and White

The Cutlass rumbled into the Sycamore Manor parking lot at quarter-to-ten. Inside the tranquil lobby, a warm Hispanic woman in her early thirties greeted Jake.

"Who are we visiting this morning?" Her eyes gave him a curious glance, as she didn't recognize the boy.

"Edith Glass, I'm Jacob Stanton, Alvin's grandson."

"Lucy got today off?" She laughed to herself. "Miss Edith will be thrilled you're here. It's wonderful of you to take her for a drive today. She simply adores her Cadillac."

"Right," Jake wondered what he'd gotten himself into.

"Since you're here, I'll have Martin bring it around to the front." She tapped away at her screen and dialed Edith to let her know of Jake's arrival. "She's ready to see you. Go down corridor eight, it's room 507."

Jake entered the main atrium, where corridors branched out like spokes on a wagon wheel. He found corridor eight and, halfway down, room 507. A sign on the door read "E. Glass" with a handwritten note taped beside it that said "Knock First."

Jacob gave two light raps.

"Who is it?" came a thin but sharp voice from inside.

"It's Jacob, Aunt Edith. Grandpa asked me to come," he began, but she cut him off mid-sentence.

"I know what I asked Alvin. Come in, please, we need to get going," she said. He heard a click, and with measured caution, he opened the door.

Edith wore a light, long-sleeved yellow blouse and

Chapter Fourteen

brown slacks. Her permed white hair framed her face and dark gray eyes seemed to pierce right through him. She was about 5'6" and a little hunched over, but not bad for someone nearing 100 years old.

"My walkers are on the dresser if you wouldn't mind getting them, please," she said as Jake took a quick look around the small apartment that was her home. He saw the dresser and her Adidas sneakers.

"Thank you for helping me get them on," she said as she sat on the bed.

"Would you like me to call for a wheelchair to take you to the car?" Jake asked as he carefully put her shoes on.

"I already called, dear, but thank you."

As she got her bag, there was a knock on the door.

"Are you ready to go, Miss E.?" came a warm, Caribbean-accented voice.

"Almost, Raymond," Edith got to her feet and moved toward the door.

"Raymond's a musician in a Ska band," Edith explained as she opened it, making introductions. "This is my great-nephew Jacob; he's going to be my driver today."

"Nice to meet you, Jacob," Raymond extended his hand, as he maneuvered beside Edith and helped her into the wheelchair.

"Good to meet you. You play Ska? That's sick. The music has such dope energy."

"It does, man."

"I play lead guitar in a band with some friends. I also do some vocals. Nothing too crazy, just rock and roll." "That's pretty fly. Ms. E. 's listened to my music; she's pretty hip, you know," Raymond gave a knowing smile.

"I've always been hip," Edith declared. "I danced to Sidney Bechet live in Chicago when I was your age, Jake. If it weren't for people like him, you wouldn't have your rock and roll."

"Wow, that's amazing! You were a flapper girl?" "Damn right, I was," Edith had a twinkle in her eye. "Your whole 'partying like it's 1999' thing has nothing on the twenties," she cackled, as Raymond let out a deep belly laugh.

Outside Jake couldn't help but admire the 1975 Fleetwood Talisman with its plush velour interior and gleaming Cotillion White paint job. He wondered how on earth he was going to maneuver this behemoth.

"Come along, Jacob. I have a schedule to keep." Raymond helped her into the passenger seat. Jake secured the wheelchair in the trunk.

Sinking into the driver's seat, Jake felt like he was enveloped in a giant, blue 1970s La-Z-Boy. It was incredibly comfortable. The steering wheel was enormous and it took a minute to adjust to it as he started the car and it rumbled to life. Taking a deep breath, Jake put the car in reverse and began to back up the land-yacht.

"So where do you want to go, Aunt Edith?"

"Didn't your grandfather give you directions?"

"He did. He actually gave me a map and directions to a couple of places." He handed Edith several pieces of paper from his pocket.

"Oh, Alvie, he always took 'Be prepared' a little too literally," Edith looked at the notes. "I'd like to go to Derek and Susan's, please. Susan knows I'm coming and Emmit's having a good day today, so I would enjoy seeing him," she said quietly before looking at Jake. "You know, that house has been in the Glass family since the 1890s. I know my nieces sold off a bunch of the acreage and now there are all these new subdivisions. But once it was just our house, surrounded by corn and soybeans as far as the eye could see."

"That's really cool," said Jake.

The drive was pleasant, passing all the fields as they headed west of Menomonee Falls. They pulled onto Glass Road, drove past the latest subdivision, and finally came up to a sunflower yellow, two-story farmhouse sitting on about five acres. As Jake maneuvered the car up the gravel drive, he pulled off to the side by the matching barn. On the porch sat his great-uncle Emmit, a spry eight-two-year-old with his Roosevelt-style

Chapter Fourteen

glasses that he'd worn since high school. His Aunt Susan sat on the porch swing.

"Remember, Jake," Edith's voice was soft yet firm, "Emmit was the youngest child of my dear sister Elizabeth. Words can't express how much I loved her. Her passing remains one of my life's unhealing scars, which is why I cherish every moment with Emmit. Family, Jake, is a thread that binds us across generations. It's our responsibility to sew each generation to the next, passing on the needle and thread, weaving each piece into the rich tapestry of our lives. You, Jake, now hold that thread. Though, I will pass on soon, and Emmit, too, I have faith that you will one day entrust it to your own grandchildren. Like the story of our lives evolve, as all things do with time, but each of us must contribute our piece. Time marches on, and the past can fade into obscurity, but it is my fervent hope that the thread of our family will continue."

A lump formed in Jake's throat as he absorbed his Aunt's words and stepped out of the car.

"Howdy, Jake!" Aunt Susan called from the porch. "Good drive?"

"Yes, it was a splendid morning drive, Susan. And how are you, Uncle Emmit?"

"I'm doing all right. But my left knee says it's gonna rain," he shot a look at Edith.

"You and your predictions, Emmit." Edith held onto the door as Jake helped her into the wheelchair. "I tell you, Jake, that boy's been thinking he's a sideshow fortune teller since before he could spell it."

Emmit flashed a wide, toothy grin. "Sometimes I've been right, Eddie."

You crazy fool," she countered. "I know, but plenty of times you've gotten the world worked up over nothing but a little wind."

As they reached the steps with the wheelchair, Jake turned to Edith, unsure about how she wanted to navigate them.

"If you can get me up so I can grab the railing, I should be alright for the five steps," she said as Jake lifted her until she could reach the railing. Susan walked her up to the porch swing. Susan went inside and returned with a large photo album, placing it between her and Edith. Jake pulled up a chair to sit opposite them as Susan opened the book and Edith carefully flipped to a page with a single picture. It was a woman in a long-sleeved gray dress, sitting on a wooden chair turned to its side. Her right hand rested gently on the chair's back, and her left hand lay in her lap, holding a rose across it.

She was beautiful in a way that defied modern descriptions. Her features were delicate, her hair a cascade of golden layers, and she wore pearl earrings. But it was her eyes that truly captured Jake's attention. They were haunting. Seemingly lost in time, yet as fresh as if they awaited their next breath of life.

"The first and last photo of Rosalind Key Glass taken as an adult," Edith ran her finger along the silver gelatin edge. "She was twenty-three at the time, and Lizzie was about three. They say Rosalind begged for Lizzie to be in the picture, but Emmit, due to your mother's lack of cooperation, it was taken without her. Instead, your grandfather gave Rosalind a single rose and pinned the brooch you see in the photograph to her chest. Apparently, they had a fight over him buying it–a good waste of sixty bucks, she supposedly remarked. That'd be like your father spending fifteen-hundred dollars and telling your mother about it afterward, Jake."

The next photo was the farm. You could see cornfields in the background and an old white horse standing by the barn. Emmit talked with Jake at length about farming back then and how long those days were. "Not like your easy desk jobs today," he stated. "Which is why, the first chance I could, I got into finance."

Edith reached over flipped to a portrait labeled '1910'. It captured four women, all dressed in their Sunday best and smiling brightly with a lake in the background that had a sloped beach that looked too familiar. One woman had dark hair and appeared to be in her late twenties. Another, with long, golden blonde hair, looked to be in her mid-twenties. There was also a

Chapter Fourteen

teenage girl with dark brown hair and another young teen with dark black hair in a pageboy cut.

"Oh my gosh, is that?" Jake stammered.

"Yes, Jake, it's all the Glass sisters together. A rare photo of us. That was taken at Bass Lake in 1910, I had just turned thirteen. Your great great-grandfather's friend Otto Beck owned land out there and Bass Lake was quite the swinging spot back then. There used to be a dance hall by the west end. They had some pretty good jazz there in the early twenties."

Edith craned her ear toward the door and listened for a moment and then turned to Susan.

"Where's Darla? I haven't had my hug yet this visit," Edith asked.

"She's upstairs, sleeping," Susan's face clouded as she looked toward the doorway. "Some days are better than others for her anymore, but that's just how it goes, I guess. She should be down at some point."

"What's wrong with her?" asked Jake, noticing the motion from Emmit to stop, but it was too late. The match was lit and a fire rose within Susan that burned with the heat of a star.

"There's nothing wrong with that child, Jake," Susan's voice moved with protectiveness. "It's the world that's wrong."

She gathered her thoughts as she sat down across from Jake.

"Sometimes, in His infinite wisdom, God graces us with a child whose heart grows far vaster than their mind or body. I believe it's His way of showing us a glimpse of what true, pure love looks like–a soul less hindered by the poisons of our humanness." Her voice broke as she reached across to clasp Edith's hand. "And she is mine."

Jake sat as the silence hung with the humidity of the air.

Emmit spoke up as he wiped his brow. "Why don't you come inside and get some tea, Eddie? Get you out of this heat."

Inside, the sitting room was furnished with a soft yellow polyester couch, love seat, and chair set, and a Grand M Steinway from the 1930s. Jake helped Edith settle into the large armchair while Emmit and Susan relaxed on the couch. Jake found himself a chair tucked away in the far corner of the room. As they enjoyed their tea, a commotion arose from upstairs. "Moooma!" a child's voice called. "Where are you, Moooma?"

"Darla, sweetheart," Susan called up. "We're downstairs. Auntie E is here."

"Eeee!" came a shout from upstairs, accompanied by footsteps thundering down the stairs. Darla burst into the front sitting room and straight into Edith's arms for a warm hug.

"I love you, Eeee!"

"I love you too, sweetheart," Edith embraced the child and her mass of waving red curls. Darla then showered her grandmother and great-grandfather with equally enthusiastic hugs. But she stopped short. The movement of her curls ceased as if she were sensing something. With wide blue eyes, she turned and fixated on Jake in the far corner for the first time.

She froze like she was seeing a ghost. Jake could see her trying to place him somehow. After a moment, she mumbled something under her breath before rushing towards him. "BoPa," she shook as she hugged him with all of her being. "You came, BoPa! You came!"

"Bopa?" Jake echoed, confused.

Her chubby hand grabbed his and led him to the old family room with a mortar stone fireplace. There, Darla pointed at a picture on the wall, her eyes sparkling with joy.

It took a moment for Jake's eyes to adjust to the dimly lit room. As they did, a wave of vertigo washed over him and uneasiness crept through his soul. Because there on the wall hung a painting–a painting of him.

Chapter Fifteen
I Cross My Heart

    The world narrowed down to simply Jake's breath and the vision before him: a painting of a man with his face, his chin, nose, and cheekbones and, more than anything, those eyes, his steel-gray eyes. It was all just too much. The only thing that brought him to a semblance of reality was the tender child hugging his legs, quietly whispering, "BoPa."
    Edith's voice broke the silence. "He was eighteen when that was done, a present from his family to capture the timeless portrait you see. The oil painting took 'Damn Near Forever,' according to my father. But the results were striking with their realism."
    "Bernard Oswald Glass was a presence to behold," Edith continued. "He was born in 1857 in Philadelphia, PA. As he used to say, four years before the world caught fire. My grandfather was in banking in the city, and Dad used to say he didn't remember much about those early years and the war. All he remembered was the perpetual talk of death. After the war was over, he spent his early education with his father in the bank and, through those dealings, he caught the eye of Rosalind Key.
    "The Key family were a big deal in Philadelphia. Not directly related to Francis Scott Key's family, but close enough that the money and power they wielded made them a priority for the bank and an important client for my grandfather. Bo, as he was called, made it known to Rosalind quite early of his interest. She, on the other hand, was coy. She was a Key. She had her pick of any man she wanted, let alone some boy whose father worked at the bank.
    "But little by little, Bo worked to create a friendship with Rosalind, and they became inseparable. He started getting into

the trade of what would become modern accounting practices and standard bookkeeping. She wasn't interested in the books as much; she was an artist. She could sing and people would stop on the street to look. She was featured in many local concerts in the area. One, for her beautiful voice and, secondly, because involving her would also allow the promoter access to the endowment of her father's money.

"My father took his training starting at seventeen at the University of Penn on the west side. After he finished his classes and was offered a full bookkeeping position in Chicago. He and Rosalind married that summer and moved to Chicago in the fall of 1879. They rented a small flat on the old Northside and shortly after their second year, Elizabeth was born."

"My mother used to say her earliest memories were going downtown with her father, for him to show her the new Home Insurance Building," Emmit said. "And she would talk at length about visiting the World's Fair in 1893. She said it was beyond-belief to explain it. There's a framed pennant that I've kept for years in the study," Emmit motioned to the back room.

"Then in 1894, he was offered the chance to open up offices in Wisconsin for farm insurance policies," Edith continued. "As part of the incentive to take it, he would be given a house and acreage as a bonus, which would become his after ten years if things went well. Obviously, he took it. The office flourished and we became farmers in the process. Dad ran the office and a few other family members came north and began our financial and agricultural adventure in Wisconsin.

"The back part of this house, to the old staircase, is where the first foundation was. There was a kitchen fire in the 1920s and the house was rebuilt to what you see today. Thankfully, he owned the land outright, and when the Great Depression hit, we all were able to ride it out, growing anything we could plant. I think he hired half the county in any way he could to help those less fortunate during those rough years."

"He passed in 1946 at eighty-nine years old," Edith said quietly. "In this very room, one summer morning. He had a rough few days with a high fever, passing in and out of consciousness.

Chapter Fifteen

We thought for sure it would take him and then, one morning, I heard him yelling. We'd all been gathered at the house, as we knew the time was close. He called out, 'Rose, is that you Rose? It's so beautiful to see you smile. I've...I've so missed you.' And then he laid back down and was silent. A few hours later, the doctor made his declaration and..."

"He was buried by the old congregational church by the water tower, laid to rest beside her," Emmit finished Edith's sentence.

"Laid next to...?" Jake questioned.

"My mother," Edith clarified. "At last, he was at peace."

They stood in silence until Edith reached for her nephew's arm, "Emmit, Susan, thank you so much for this afternoon."

Jake added, "Yes, thank you for today," as they walked to the sitting room.

Jake was about to head out to get the wheelchair ready when Darla, who had been silent for the last few minutes, walked over to Edith.

"Eee," she said softly as Edith carefully sat and the child crawled up and kissed her. Jake watched as she clutched her hand to her own chest and pressed it on Edith ever so gently, then hugged and kissed her.

Then she turned to Jake, asking in a soft voice, "BoPa, want my love?"

Jake wasn't sure what she meant or if he had heard her correctly. "Darla, what do you want?" he kneeled down to the floor so he could look into her eyes.

A tenderheartedness glowed in her eyes. "BoPa, you want my love?"

"Yes, I do."

Darla rushed into Jake's arms for a hug and then stepped back. She kissed her hands, held them to her chest, and looked deeply into Jake's eyes. Leaning in, she placed her hands on his chest, mirroring her earlier gesture with Edith.

The innocence and love in her soul stirred something deep within Jake. He saw a purity that transcended the complexities of the world. When she looked at him again, a hint of concern flickered in her eyes.

"BoPa," she whispered. "Can I have your love?"

Jake's heart swelled. The pain from his mother's indifference and lack of acceptance, coupled with the fresh sting of Marta's rejection and his heart still torn by Bonnie, all seemed insignificant compared to the childlike innocence before him. This wasn't a demand for toys or gifts, but a simple, profound request for love.

Emotion choked Jake's voice. A single "Yes," escaped his lips. He cupped his hands together, kissed them, then pressed them to his heart before placing them over hers.

Darla said nothing, but in her eyes came a tear of joy. "I love you, BoPa," she mouthed as she embraced him with all her being.

"I love you too, Darla, with all my heart," he whispered, as all the pain of the unwanted love walled within his soul emptied in that moment, to the heart of a child this world was not worthy of.

Chapter Sixteen
Flesh N Blood

December 22, 1991, Tucson, AZ - 6 Months Earlier

"You had no right!" Jake stormed into the west wing of the sprawling stucco ranch a brisk December's walk from the Finger Rock trailhead. The strains of "White Christmas" that carried from the patio were lost on the boy, who pointed a shaky finger at his mother. Cindy's steel expression was unmoved as she tapped her SuperSlim in the cactus-shaped ashtray, and took a sip of her Pineapple Slice.

"How about you lower your voice and start with at least a 'Hello'," her voice laced with disgust as she glared back at her son. "By the way, I'm glad you graced us with your presence. Lunch was scheduled for noon." She turned her wrist and glanced at her Pearlmaster. "It's nearly three."

"I would have been here earlier if I hadn't gotten a call from Matt's dad saying he was cutting me from the winter travel team due to scheduling conflicts mid-season." Jake paced, his eyes never leaving his mother. The alcohol-covered island acted as a natural barrier. "Conflicts that were complete news to me. I can't even begin to say how embarrassed I am." He waved his arm and grabbed a Keystone Light out of the ice bucket center island. He cracked it open and took a swig, his eyes never leaving hers.

"I spent two hours digging up the same story, except the source of it. The name that never got mentioned, but hinted at, was you. So, seriously! What gives? If I'm going to look good for scouts this spring, I need to be in the best form possible and have all the wrinkles worked out before I even step on the field. I'm wondering why?"

"Why – what?" a graveled voice from the opposite doorway asked. "I'll tell you Jake. What I've been wondering is where my grandson was who didn't have the common courtesy to show up for Christmas dinner. I'm wondering why, too?" Andrew poured himself a shot of Wild Turkey on the rocks as he studied the boy.

"Sorry I missed lunch, Grandpa."

Andrew humphed to himself at this initial comment, his face showing his age and a keen wit that hadn't aged a bit.

"I lost track of time," Jake tried to plead his case. "I called around and got a friend. I won't say who because I don't want any retaliation against them," Jake moved like a tiger glaring through glass at his mother. "But I was told that, on Wednesday, an update was faxed to the league office by my parents. Grandpa, Here's the weird thing. Dad was flying all day Wednesday to get here for the holidays. But my mother has a fax machine right on her desk in the accounting department of your company."

"That's enough of this." Cindy ground the smoldering butt into the ashtray, her eyes lingered on the Chardonnay as she took another sip of her Slice.

"Not for me." Andrew leaned against the marble counter and swirled the ice in his glass. "Please continue."

Jake's voice rose in anger, "My own mother used her influence and faxed a letter of complete lies to crush my ability to play in the winter league. I know Mom hates baseball, but why would she go to all that trouble to remove me from the league entirely without telling me?"

Cindy bristled as she lit another cigarette. "Before you start, Dad, this is none of your business," She took a long drag and blew the smoke toward her father.

She shifted her posture to Jake, spitting each word. "And you, Jacob, are way out of line. Someone needed to step in and do what you don't have the sense to do yourself. You forced my hand to intervene."

"Actually," Andrew interjected as he raised a finger, gaze fixed on Cindy, "Since you used my company's hours, building, and even my fax to conduct your little scheme, I'm curious.

Chapter Sixteen

What was so urgent that it required billing me?"

Cindy's face flushed with anger. "If you must know, Dad," she snapped, "This boy didn't take any AP classes this fall and he refused – refused! – to switch to any this spring. No honors classes because, *God forbid*, the extra work affect his precious baseball or that ridiculous band he plays in. His grades are pitiful and he needs volunteer work if he's going to get into Stanford. No scholarship or legacy-admittance are happening without a check I'd rather not have to write."

"Stanford?" Jake was exasperated. "This again? I don't want to go to Stanford! I want to go to a Big-Ten school, play baseball, major in sports management or business event management, and get out of this state for good. That's my dream, and what I—"

"What you want?" Cindy cut him off again. "Sorry, son, but to quote the song, 'You can't always get what you want' – especially if I'm paying for it."

"So it's about *your* money?" Jake shot back, his voice contorted with frustration. "Fine, I don't want it. I still can't believe you did this. It's crazy, Grandpa," he turned to Andrew. "What do you think?"

Cindy's finger crumpled into the soda can. "Dad, I don't want to hear—",

Andrew raised his hand, "Cindy, you don't have to hear me out on how to parent, but since this situation involves me – as, last I checked, I believe it's still my company and I'm the one who wrote a rather nice check to the league this fall – I will answer the question." He turned back to his grandson, "Jake. I agree with you, it isn't fair and, frankly, I don't think your mother handled this appropriately." His eyes darted back at this daughter.

"Just curious, Cindy, before I hear it third-hand, was my name used to get your dirty work done? For your sake, I hope not.

"As for you, Jake, winter ball is a lost cause at this point. But your spring season isn't. Use the extra time to condition on your own." He leaned back against a barstool. "I've heard your grades aren't reflecting your full potential. However, I will say this: if there's anything your mother has signed you up for that you don't approve of, I'll back you with your father to get you out of it, as long as your grades improve."

"Yes, sir."

"Dad, don't promise things you can't back up," Cindy's eyes flickered with her cigarette.

"Before you get hasty, darling, about what I can and can't back up, I'd double check what I'm already backing," a cold edge lined his voice.

"Fine," Cindy's eyes narrowed at Jake. "Winter ball is dead. Can we all agree on that? I don't want to hear another word about it. However, community service is a must. Every college looks for that," she pushed back.

Andrew's eyes sparked with an idea. "And I know the perfect setup for the boy. I've been wanting to get more involved with Scott at Habitat for Humanity. I'll go along and work with Jake to make sure he gets it done. It'll be good quality time for us and he can learn a few trade skills as well. Those will never hurt him down the road. That sound like a fair compromise?"

"Sounds good, Grandpa," Jake replied. "Mom?"

Cindy fumed from the inside out, but the battle was over. "For now. But I want to see action behind his words, Dad. Grades have to come up."

"Agreed," Andrew said. "Now, let's put down our guns, find a smile, and join the party. It's Christmas, God dammit!" he spat as he left the room to rejoin his guests.

Chapter Sixteen

Jacob's drive back with Aunt Edith had been filled with more wonderful stories. Raymond met them at the front of Sycamore Manor and helped his Aunt get to dinner and took care of the Caddy. Jake said goodbye to his aunt, telling her he looked forward to seeing her next Thursday.

As he unlocked the door and entered the house, it was dark. The only sounds were the excited pitter-patter of Maggie rushing to greet him with happy snorts. He ruffled the little dog's fur as he made his way to the kitchen and checked the fridge. There, stuck to the door, was a yellow note:

Jacob's stomach lurched. He sighed, the dread of the coming storm settling on him. He opened the fridge to find the casserole dish of cheeseburger mac and reheated a plateful in the microwave, his mind already churning with the inevitable confrontation with his mother.

Chapter Seventeen
No Son of Mine

Upstairs, Jake looked at the cordless phone, the dread building in his stomach like the dry-heave of three-day flu. He sat on the couch as he took the phone from the cradle, pulled out his calling card, and punched in the numbers. The phone rang twice then clicked as he heard the warm voice of his mother.

"Hello," hit his ears, her office voice still turned on. "This is Cindy Stanton."

"Hey, Mom," His voice sounded like he was eleven and it was a Thursday afternoon in June. "Grandpa left a note that—"

"That I called three hours ago," Cindy cut him off, her voice turning the conversation as cold as an open door in winter.

"I just got home. I was out—" he stammered.

"Oh, I'm sure you were 'out'," she scoffed. "I talked with Evelyn, she told me you've already been 'out' twice with the Cloud girl."

"Bonnie, Oh my God, Mom, she's—" he clenched his fist, his voice raw, "I was with Aunt Edith all day, Grandpa should have told you that."

"I didn't talk with Alvin long, son. We have a mutual understanding that works best for both of us. But, no matter, the reason I called is because I got a call from Christopher Carroll at Carroll and Brown." Her manicured nails clacked on the countertop, a countdown to detonation.

"You never scheduled with him before you left, not even a damn note." Disgust spat through the phone. "You can do whatever you want on your own time, but when it affects my reputation—"

"Do what? An interview that doesn't—" he tried to reply.

"Doesn't matter," she barked. "It doesn't matter? It's

They Say It's a River 97

Chapter Seventeen

your alumni interview for applying to Stanford. It is required. Unbelievable, you..." She rapped the receiver against the counter.

The voice that returned was one he had banished to the recesses of his brain and nights in his closet. "You have to do it. I took the time to set that up. I even had lunch with the man to field all his questions about you and ensure that your interview went smoothly no matter what nonsense you might say."

Jake felt the verbal slap. "I know how to do an interview. God knows I've seen you do enough of them. But I don't want to go to Stanford, I don't want to major in Business or try to get into Grad School."

"I don't care what you want!" Her temper clawed at the reins of her sobriety. "It's about the future – and your place in it."

"What if I don't want—" He interjected.

"Don't want what? A future?" Cindy was stupefied. "You're just a kid. You have no clue what you want, or an idea about the realities of life."

"What are you talking about, I have—" Jake attempted to get back into the conversation.

"Stop it!"

Jake flinched in muscle memory, forgetting she wasn't there.

"Let me explain one very simple rule, little boy," her voice slowed as she nuanced through each word as if she were stringing pearls. "She who has the gold makes the rules. And in case you have forgotten, I have the gold."

"I don't want it," he said, barely audible.

"Speak up, Jacob! If you want to be treated like a man, learn to enunciate," Cindy hissed.

"I don't want it!" Jake shouted, louder than intended.

"Found your tongue, have you?" Her laugh cut deep. "What exactly don't you want? Can't wait to write the list."

"Why are you like this?" His voice was thick with hurt. "Why can't I pick where I go, who my friends are, or if I play baseball or not? I don't get it. You've never cared."

Jake winced at the unmistakable crash of the phone being

No Son of Mine

hurled and the ricocheting off the wall, the line crackling with static and bumped dial tones. There was a pause, an eerie silence, interrupted by approaching footsteps and indistinguishable curses. He was a repeat audience to this show. He gripped the phone and waited.

The voice returned, "What did you say?"

"Why don't you care?" His voice was flat.

"I care, Jacob. I care about our business, I care about our future, and I care about where you belong within it. Don't... you...dare...question...that," Cindy searched for calm in her voice.

"Two months and I'm eighteen," The pain mixed with defiance in his words. "You won't be able to control me anymore."

"Control you? That's how you see it?" Cindy scoffed. "Let me make this perfectly clear, Jacob. That door swings only one way. Think long and hard before you open that one, Pandora."

"I'd do it," he muttered, more to himself than her.

"You ungrateful child!" There was a loud crash–something heavy thrown across the room–and the line went dead.

Jake sat in the silence. He knew this performance all too well. His heart and mind buzzed as he awaited for the impending encore, the song choice still to be decided.

Five minutes passed before the phone rang again. His hand trembled, hitting the speaker button on the third ring.

"I should put you on a plane tomorrow and drag your ass back home, your little escapades be damned."

"I won't go."

"Are you threatening me?" Cindy sucked in a breath for her finale.

"Be careful what you wish for, Jacobee," she taunted as if he was five. "You've forgotten. I *always* get what I want." And the line went dead again.

Jake released his grasp on the receiver as it fell to the floor. His heart raced, his mind on fire. The reality finally hit

Chapter Seventeen

him. She truly didn't care. His hopes and dreams meant nothing. Nothing in her world held more importance than her relentless pursuit of the next thing – the next merger, the next cocktail party, the next profile to bolster her reputation. He was either a pawn in her game or a piece to be discarded.

He looked out the window at the darkness and released a primal scream of the emotions that churned within him. He yelled until his voice gave out, the raw pain and abandonment threatening to consume him. Exhausted, he collapsed on the couch and pulled the old, ragged turtle blanket from his childhood summers around him. He curled beneath it and wept himself to sleep.

Chapter Eighteen
Love is a Battlefield

DING
"Fries are done," Clara called to Leah.
"Do you want an apple pie with that?" Bonnie looked over the register at the lanky man, whose eyes were wandering the pastries in the glass case.
"You got any of that Strawberry Rhubarb left?" John Stanley asked, glad he had remembered this question before he had gotten home.
Bonnie noticed the lack of one behind the glass. "Grandma?"
"What, dear?" She moved so Leah could salt the fries and made her way to the counter.
"Do we have any strawberry rhubarb?"
"Sometimes," when she saw it was John, her thoughts went to the answer to another question. "Oh, hey John, was Susan looking for a whole pie?"
"Yes and, Clara, any chance of a whole pie before Sunday?"
"For you, John, I can make a special order. Bonnie, remind me later that the Stanley's want a pie to pick up on Saturday afternoon," Clara said before turning her attention back to the conversation. "And, John, let Susan know I said I look forward to her help at the women's auxiliary next Tuesday," Clara winked.
"I will, thank you, Clara," John grabbed his sack of burgers and fries, as he headed out he wondered how to tell his wife what the true cost of that pie she had to have was.
Leah was stopping to catch her breath as she opened a box of styrofoam cups in the back before she heard it again:

Chapter Eighteen

DING

"Fries are done," called Clara.

"Coming. I'm grabbing more cups," Leah replied.

"Thank you, dear," said Clara as she took the cups from Leah and began restacking them by the soda fountain.

Bonnie waved to her grandmother, as they headed out the backdoor of the diner, another shift in the books. The light breeze of the lake took a nice edge off the humidity on their stroll down the dirt road.

At the farmhouse, Leah sprawled herself on the porch swing and Bonnie brought out an iced tea, quenching her thirst.

"That looks so good." Leah's throat longed for something cool.

"You gonna just take it." Bonnie shot her a look, no longer talking about tea.

"Bonnie, come on, I am so worn out, are we hashing this out again."

"I have no idea what you're referring to." She sipped her tea with great pleasure.

"Fine, I'll get my own." Leah got off the swing and with annoyance went into the house.

Bonnie rubbed her tired feet, sinking deeper into the chair beside the swing. Her gaze drifted toward the lake, its surface shimmering as the breeze rippled through the trees. She tried to ground herself, but the ache in her chest didn't fade.

Jake Stanton. Just thinking his name made her stomach twist. She knew what she had before her today. The words she had rehearsed in the mirror since their night at the drive in and the urgency that Leah would give her the chance to say it.

Leah returned with her tea in a large teal tupperware tumbler. "It's almost one. Think the guys are still out fishing?"

"My grandpa and Jakes' would fish until they ran out of bait and even then they'd still sit out in the boat smoking and talking 'til dark," Bonnie looked out toward the lake. "Why?"

"I'm wondering how much time I've got, as I want to clean up a little," Leah shook out her hair from under her Braves cap.

"Really?" Bonnie's irritation snipped at her cousin. "You know you could throw that wheat sack by the barn on and shove your hair in my work bandana and that boy would still follow you around like the stinkin' pied piper."

"You think so?" Leah caught the frown from Bonnie and decided to let it go. "That whole staying here at the lake. You think he's gonna be allowed to live out here?"

"If you have any wild ideas in that head of yours, a reminder: see the little green cottage with the peaked roof and off-center upstairs window just at the start of the curve in the road. That's Stanton's place. There are 468 people that live in Bass Lake and my grandmother knows all of them and their business."

"Okay, I'll be careful, but you didn't answer my question."

"I don't know. Jake often has lots of fantastic dreams in his head but misses on the delivery. He'll push but not too much."

"Why not?"

"Jake is terrified of the women in his family."

"Really, he's afraid of who?"

"His Aunt Evelyn, his grandmother, 'cause she runs the show for that family, and, lastly, there is Cindy May Stanton, his mother. She is a force of nature. If you get to meet her, you'll see," Bonnie flatly replied

"So, what are the plans for the afternoon?"

"You and I have both been invited to lunch with the Stantons, per Gram."

"Oh," said Leah. "So why do you keep watching their cottage if they ain't there?"

"They should be arriving any minute now and I'm watching for Lucy and Evelyn to come out of the van with Natalie and Brian. Then I'll know how the day is going by seeing one thing."

"What's that?" asked Leah.

"If they bring the pug. If Lucy and Evelyn are not ready

Chapter Eighteen

to murder each other or the world, they will bring the pug. If they show up with no dog, no dice."

"Hmm, you know them pretty well?"

"I've been watching that mother-daughter dynamic longer than I can remember, cuz, and those two women are as easy to read as a five-o'clock shadow."

They enjoyed the cool breeze until they saw a minivan pull up to the green cottage. Evelyn busied herself with getting the food inside, Natalie and Brian assisting her. Lucy got out of the van and opened the rear passenger door, half-disappearing for a minute. Moments later, a small ball of fawn fur hopped down and ran in a badly-drawn figure eight around the van until she was scooped up by Natalie. Her grandmother put a leash on the dog and headed into the cottage.

"There's our cue." Bonnie got up and headed into the house. Inside, Bonnie stopped at the staircase, her hand gripping the banister. "Leah," she called out, the scratches in her voice causing Leah to stop.

"What's up?" Leah turned, her eyes curious as the weight pressing down on Bonnie became apparent. "Are you okay?"

Bonnie hesitated, her lips parting but no words coming out at first. She looked at Leah and felt an envy that made her ashamed—a wish for that which she didn't have. "No."

Leah sat on the step, lost within the storm that brewed below her. "Bonnie, I'm not a mind reader."

Bonnie's throat tightened. "I want you to promise me something."

"What's that?"

Bonnie's fingers brushed the wooden railing as if it could somehow ground her at that moment. "Just one day," she raised her eyes to her cousin. "Just me and Jake. No molasses-thick Southern charm or smoky batted eyelashes hypnotizing him into a trance. Just come, enjoy lunch, and then head back here to take a nap. Please." Her voice trembled around the edges as she struggled to steady it. She didn't want to beg, but with Leah's eyes, she could see the understanding of her request.

Leah blinked, caught a little off-guard by Bonnie's words,

but they hit home. "Okay," Leah relented, her tone softening. "I promise. No flirting."

Bonnie moved up the steps and pulled Leah into a quick hug. "Thank you," she whispered, letting go. Leah made her way up the stairs to change. Bonnie, unmoved, looked out the windows at the lake.

She walked out to the front porch, her bare feet scuffing against the weathered wood. The light breeze was nothing compared to the storm within her heart.

Her memories flashed as she looked toward the hayloft. She could still see him strumming songs on the acoustic guitar, pouring out words from the darkness of his world. She knew the weight he carried, the worries he had, and the fears he faced. The world saw Jake Stanton as the spoiled rich kid who had the world on a string, but Bonnie knew the little boy hiding after bad dreams in a closet.

Her hand tightened against the porch post, her knuckles white. Bonnie had tried to hate Jake when he went after Marta and shattered her heart, but she couldn't. Not when every letter he wrote to her during those long winters still brought her back to here. Through all the years, she couldn't imagine a world where Jake Stanton didn't exist within her life. But imagining wasn't enough. Not anymore.

She closed her eyes as she mouthed through the words she had practiced a hundred times, each one a piece of her heart that she'd hand over, not to be taken back.

"I need to tell you something," she murmured under her breath, testing the words as much as her voice. Then she repeated, a little louder, "Jake, I need to tell you something." She pressed the heel of her hand against the corner of her eyes to push back the emotions of her heart.

"I'll tell him," she whispered within her soul. "And then I'll let him go."

It was the only way.

Even if it broke her.

Chapter Nineteen
Fish On

Alvin looked at Harold as he puffed on his cigar, "You think we got enough in the basket?"

"Depends on what your goal is for that basket? A little bit for lunch or are you thinking of an actual fish fry? 'Cause for that, we're a little short."

"Oh, mainly freezing. I'll keep them on ice 'til I clean them later. The women should have lunch ready when we get back. And once Lucy has a plan in motion, I usually let it ride, you know, Harold."

"Yup. If they have it all planned out, just go with the flow. You'll learn that someday, Jacob."

"Learn what?" Jacob recast his line from the front of the boat.

"How to keep the women from getting all riled up," Harold advised, placing a new worm on his hook.

"Something you could probably learn a little better," Alvin looked in the worm container Harold had passed him. "Currently, son, you have your aunt and grandmother chasing windmills over your push to stay here at the cottage, and your mother sounded pretty fired up herself when I talked to her last night."

"She sure was," Jake looked out over the bow. "She's not happy with me right now."

"Jacob," Alvin cleared his throat and took a drag from his stogie. "I don't think your mother is ever gonna be happy with what she can't control. I feel for you, son, but, that's where it is."

"On a different note," Harold recast closer to the shore, before tapping his cigar in the makeshift tray mid-boat, "I heard the full discussion this morning. You've got those two stirred up like a bag of hornets."

"Really?" Jake could only imagine, after the other night with Bonnie.

"They are planning something for this afternoon. Just behave yourself."

"Yes," Alvin looked at his grandson. "Behave."

"I will, Grandpa. Don't worry."

"Jacob, just remember, I was seventeen once," he glanced at his watch. "Well, it's almost quarter after; Lucy said lunch was at two, so we probably should start heading back. Jake, can you get the anchor up?"

"Sure, Grandpa," Jake stowed his pole and started pulling in the rope that was hanging over the bow.

Soon they were motoring across the lake, the old men enjoying the last of their cigars that would be shunned back at the cottage. As they neared the dock, Natalie was already out with Maggie, who was staring out at the water and barking at a passing boat and water skier.

"Oh good, they brought Maggie," Alvin thought out loud.

Maggie appeared, leaning into the boat to investigate the catch of the day.

"Maggie, go with Jacob, please. Leave the fish alone," he instructed the dog, who snorted an indignant reply, but followed Jake out as Alvin and Harold finished unloading the boat.

"Hey Jake," Natalie walked with Jake across the grass. "You guys catch much?"

"A few nice perch and a couple bass, but nothing crazy."

"No fish stories?"

"No, but definitely heard a few."

"Come up to the house and help me get lunch ready. Gram and Mom have enough fried chicken, mashed potatoes, and sides to feed an army."

"I know Bonnie and Leah may stop—"

"Oh, I heard all about it on the drive here. What is going on with you?" asked Natalie.

Chapter Nineteen

"I'll," he started to say, then saw his Aunt coming out from the porch. "I'll tell you later," he glanced toward his aunt.

Evelyn was wiping her hands in a dishtowel as she motioned to them. "Jacob, glad you boys are back. Give me a hand and we'll have lunch here in a few. And help me tidy up as we have company coming. This cottage is a mess," she said as she returned back to her cleaning.

Jake headed into the house with Natalie and began cleaning up.

Leah and Bonnie were packing the last few items in their bag, as Leah took another look in the mirror. "This look okay?" she asked, tugging her lemon-yellow shorts down a little to make sure they came closer to her knee, leaving the GoodFellas T-shirt untucked. Bonnie adjusted her beret, which complimented the jean shorts and floral tee she wore over her swimsuit.

"You look marvelous," she answered in her best Joe Pesci impression, double checking her own bag as they walked out the door.

"So, is it a lunch on the level of an inquisition or afternoon social?" asked Leah.

"You and I might be given some level of interrogation. The only one in the line of fire will be Jake. Those women are gonna be watching for any signs that 'unsettle their souls' about Jake being out here by himself."

"So, go with the usual? Vague answers and lots of smiles?"

"Yes, It shouldn't be too bad."

"Evelyn and Lucy will just want to chat you up. It won't get too over the top, as my grandma would have it out with Lucy if it got too personal." Bonnie turned to face Leah and took her hand. "After lunch, Jake and I will head out. I appreciate you understanding how much I need today."

"I get it." Leah squeezed her hand. "It's gonna be okay."

Bonnie knocked on the door as Lucy opened it with a face full of smiles. "Oh, Bonnie, you are looking more like your momma everyday." Lucy pulled her in for a hug.

Fish On

"Thank you, Mrs. Stanton. It's good to see you."

"Yes, come in, dear, out of the heat. And you must be Leah. How are you doing, dear? I'm Mrs. Stanton." She gave Leah a big hug. "My heart goes out to you. Know that you always have an open door here."

"Thank you," Leah whispered as she hugged Lucy and went into the house. There was a long table set up on the screened-in porch. Harold, Alvin, Natalie, Jake, and Brian were there, with open seats between Harold and Jake on the far side of the table. Bonnie sat down next to grandpa and Leah took a seat next to Jake. "Hi, Grandpa," Bonnie leaned in, giving him a hug.

"Afternoon, Bee. Leah. Thanks for helping your Grandma this morning, and letting me go fishing."

"No problem, grandpa. It was busy."

"That's good. Is she doing okay? Did the boys get there on time?"

"Yeah, she's doing fine, and the boys got there at one p.m.," answered Bonnie.

"They should hold things down until they close. Besides, if not, she knows where to find us. She may come over here in a little while; we shall see. The boys can handle the place by themselves."

"Hey, Farmer Tan." Leah gave just enough southern charm to attract Bonnie's attention, but not too much to start a fight.

"Hi, Leah." Jake blushed a little when she called him that in front of everyone.

"Farmer Tan?" Alvin laughed. "Young lady, I like you already."

There was a knock at the door, and Clara appeared with Lucy, Evelyn, and Natalie carrying plates of fried chicken, mashed potatoes, green beans, and other sides.

Lunch was now in full session with laughter and talk of the morning's fishing.

As the meal wound down, Evelyn could no longer restrain herself. "Leah, I am so glad you could join us for lunch. I've heard bits and pieces from your Aunt. So how are you liking

Chapter Nineteen

Wisconsin?"

"It's a nice change. It's much cooler than Atlanta," Leah answered, looking for a safe topic.

"I'm sure," Lucy added, not waiting to be left out of the conversation. "Hopefully, you're getting a chance to relax and get away from it all."

"Yes, it's nice to get a break from..." Leah caught Lucy's eye. "Everything."

Lucy nodded with a kind smile. "So, what are your plans for the next couple of weeks?"

"Well, I think that's mostly up to Bonnie. She has the wheels. I know we have some days planned at the farm and I think I saw our name pretty regularly on the schedule at the diner," she said with a wry grin at her grandparents.

"Oh, I'm sure. Never like to see a child ever risk boredom, do we Clara?" he joked to his wife.

"Oh, don't I know it," chuckled Bonnie, as she started helping Natalie and Jake clear the plates from the table.

"Hey, Jake," said Bonnie. "Is the Sunfish still in the other bay of the boathouse?" She asked as they entered the kitchen.

"Yeah," said Jake. "Why?"

"I don't know, do you want to take it out? There's a nice breeze, and it's not supposed to be too bad of weather. We didn't take it out at all last summer."

"Sure, we could do that." Jake thought for a second. "Leah, will you be okay if just Bonnie and I head out?"

"No, that's fine, Jake." She caught a sidelong look from her cousin and faked a yawn. "I'm pretty tired from this morning and I didn't sleep well last night. I may go back to the farm and take a nap."

"Have a good afternoon, Leah. I'm gonna head down and get the boat rigged up. Come on down when you're ready, Bonnie."

"Aye, aye, Captain," she winked to Leah as they parted and Jake headed out to the boathouse.

Chapter Twenty
Hold On My Heart

The roll-up door of the boathouse clanged against the rollers and shook some rust out of the tracks and onto Jake's head. He zipped his shirt in the dry bag and tossed it, and two life jackets, in the boat. With his board shorts on, he was ready to sail. Hopping into the water, he drifted the sailboat out into the open water before securing it to the dock. After raising the mast and sail, he set to work on prepping the rigging. Once complete, he donned his life jacket and ran through his mental checklist before setting sail.

He looked up to see Bonnie approaching in her new sherbet-striped one-piece, her hair flowing freely in the breeze.

Jake let out a low whistle, "Looking pretty fly, first mate."

Bonnie's ears burned. "Well, I'm glad you like it. She sashayed up to the dock and winked at Jake. "Ready to go, Captain?"

"As long as my first mate is." He reached up, helping her into the boat. They untied it and raised the sail into the breeze. Jake manned the tiller while Bonnie steadied the lines and they glided out into the crystal water. They rounded the north shore before tacking left, through the channel and into the vast second half of the lake. After navigating the channel, they crossed back over to the south shore. Jake spotted a clearing and felt the wind pick up.

"Prepare to tack!" he called. Bonnie ducked and adjusted the line as the wind began to dance in the sail, bringing it to life. They skimmed across the water with a slight heel to the right as Bonnie giggled and held on. Her laughter filled the air as they zig-zagged across the lake. Heading along the southern shore, Jake felt a slight shift in the wind.

Chapter Twenty

"Prepare to come about!" he called as they turned and made their way back towards the channel and then tacked to the northern shallow bay. Bulrushes and pickerelweed lined the shallow shoreline. A small clearing formed a sand beach on the edge of the Swensen's farm, adjacent to the lake. A little yellow picnic table and sandstone fire pit sat near a large red maple with a tire swing that Bonnie and Jake had used over the summers with Nole and Maja Swensen.

"Want to go to the beach for a while and swim in the bay?" Bonnie suggested.

"Sure," Jake was rather warm, himself, and a dip in the cool water sounded refreshing. He feathered the rudder as they glided in. Bonnie hopped out to help ease the boat onto the sand. Jake pulled off his life jacket and dove into the water. Bonnie was quickly behind him. They floated, relaxing in the water.

Bonnie drifted closer to him and, with a slap on his back, yelled, "Tag!" and rocketed away.

"No fair, Miss Swimteam," yelled Jake as he butterflied in the water and raced after her. After twenty minutes of being far-outmatched, Jake neared the shore to catch his breath. He walked up the sand and leaned back on the table. Bonnie sat beside him and they relaxed their winded bodies.

A few minutes of silence passed, breathing the only sound between them. Bonnie glanced at Jake and moved her leg over the bench so she could face him directly. "Jake, about the other night."

Jake was focused on a boat with two skiers skimming across the water near the channel. "What?" he replied without looking her way.

When she didn't answer, Jacob turned to see her eyes, which seemed to hold a weight she no longer wished to carry. "Bonnie, what's wrong?"

She pulled up next to him, looking him directly in the eye, her dark blue eyes gleaming. "Jake, this is our seventh summer together," she said, clearing her throat. "And the last chapter of this time in our lives."

He frowned, shaking his head. "Come on, Bonnie.

Hold On My Heart

Seriously? You don't know that."

She swallowed back a dozen answers that wouldn't say enough. "Jake, stop and actually listen to me," her voice trembled as she scooted just close enough so her knee touched the outside of his. "And, just this once," she moved her hand till it found the right side of his chest. "With your heart."

Her hand was cool to the touch, but her eyes held a warmth that Jake hadn't seen look into his own for some time.

She could feel his heart under her palm, beating with hers, but not for it. "Jake, I need to tell you something I haven't told you in a long time and maybe I should have told you sooner. But, this past year and a half, my heart's been a mess. You've been a part of my life and my summers for as long as I can remember." She pointed out toward the cottage and diner on the far shore. "Seeing you walk up that road became something I looked forward to each year as much as Christmas but, in a way, more. Because you being here meant summer was, too. Our summer. You were my escape from the microscope of this small town's scrutiny."

Jake looked into her eyes as his right hand slipped into her left. Bonnie steadied herself and squeezed his hand as they wrapped their fingers.

"Because you always got the green light with my mom and grandma, we could just go. Those endless days and nights, from kids goofing off to that last summer, when I felt it blooming into something more. I know you didn't feel the same way. You said you loved me three years ago and I know you didn't push for anything because you didn't want to hurt me and because of your own fears. Your fear of the distance, the difference in our backgrounds, the fear of our families, and the fear of…" She lifted her hand from his heart to his cheek and wiped away a tear. "The secrets you carried for so long, the truth of why you were here."

Bonnie looked away as her heart struggled with how things had changed.

"And then, you went after Marta. I sat on the sidelines and watched as she took your heart, bartered for all it was worth

Chapter Twenty

and, when it was spent, she tossed it away. I wept for you because you've always had a piece of mine." Bonnie's words scratched at Jake's heart as she held his hand.

"Jake, I love you and I probably always will. You know, in the last two years, I've learned to love someone else, but fate is far crueler than I would wish. And though I love Raff and he loves me, he's stationed in a war zone on the other side of the world and, from what he told me last, he's probably not coming back for a long time. I know he'd like to, but I don't know if it's meant to be."

"So, when you wrote me that Marta had finally broken your heart for the last time and that you would be here for a full month, I don't know, I thought that maybe somehow, with you planning to choose a different path and walking away from what is expected of you in life, that there would be a place for me within it. But I struggled with what to say, or even if to say it. So the other night…" She stopped, the sting of it still fresh in her heart.

"Bonnie, you are the reason I have always come back here. You and this place were my escape too. What do you want me to say."

"Nothing." Bonnie pulled her face close to his. "I know you care for me Jake and I'm one of the closest friends you have in this world, but that's just it."

She reached and touched her hands to his lips. "The words from your mouth miss the eight inches to your heart." She pulled his hand over her own heart. "So here I am, sharing mine. Not to hurt you, but to tell you that, no matter where you are, I will always love you. And I love you enough to let you go."

Her voice stopped, the ripple of sail the only sound between them. Jake was shaken more by her words than if she had hit him with the dagger board. "Bonnie, I—'"

"Shh," she said. Jake pulled her close and held her.

Chapter Twenty-One
Just a Friend

"Bonnie, would you please tell me what's going on with you?" Leah toyed with the yellow sunglasses that wouldn't stay up in her hair. "You and Jake disappear for hours until both your grandparents practically send out a search party at twilight. Then, you two show up at the cottage. Not by boat, but dropped off in a Mercedes-Benz, all sunburnt and acting goofy, like two drunks. What the heck?"

Bonnie stared out at the night sky."I'm good. I made Jake promise one day of just us and he kept it. Leah, we haven't had a day together like that in over two years." Her voice was wistful. "I've so missed—"

"I can guess what you've missed."

"Oh my God, Lee, not like that! Jeez!" Bonnie exclaimed. "I've missed him so much. Jake knows more about my life than anyone. The major events, he was there for them or he's the person I told about them. Ever wonder how my cursive got so pretty? It's because I've spent years, since fifth grade, crafting letters to that boy, as open and long as my diary, probably even longer. Poor guy. I remember him writing back confused in the fall of seventh grade about me telling him I got my first period. And he wrote, not getting the big deal, saying everyone has first period in middle school."

"That's hysterical."

"I can't remember what I wrote back to him, but he never brought it up in any letters after that."

"You probably scarred him for life."

"Probably, but that's just it. We were like siblings, at least to him and, yet, I saw it as more. So..." Bonnie slowed as they came to the interstate onramp. "This afternoon, I told him."

Chapter Twenty-One

"Wait, stop," Leah's mouth dropped as she sorted her thoughts. "You told him what?"

"I told him how I've felt,"

"Wow, and?"

"It really changed the rest of the afternoon. The tension was gone. So we decided to relive all our favorites from the past."

"Where did you go?"

"We went over and docked at the Porter's Club and had lunch. Krissy's dad is the general manager. She was hanging out with Dylan and his friends joined us after lunch. We headed over to Krissy's and the lake wasn't too busy with boat traffic. Krissy dug around in their boathouse and found a second pair of water skis. Her and I haven't dual skied in forever."

"Did Jake try?"

"No. Jake knows enough to keep his weight back and when to straighten his legs, but not much beyond that. He and the boys had a blast driving the Bowrider and catching up. Then we got out the jet skis until we ended up at Dylan's grandparents' cottage for dinner."

"Have I met them?"

"Yes, Mrs. Morrison is a regular."

"Morrison." Leah's face lit up as she placed the name. "Does she have the Elizabeth-Taylor bangs and no concept of personal space?"

"That's her, but she makes the best moussaka you ever had," Bonnie laughed. "After dinner we played cards there until the sun was starting to go down. That's when Mrs. Morrison's phone rang. It was my grandmother, saying she had called the Porter's Club and Krissy's dad told her where we were. So, Mr. Morrison gave us a lift back to the cottage."

"You know, Jake is probably getting grilled right now."

"Actually, you'd be wrong," Bonnie replied. "We've been doing this since middle school. Not always intentionally. We'd get the sailboat on a good wind and take it all the way to the far side of the northwest part of the lake, past the channel. Back then, we weren't skilled enough to get the boat back if the wind wasn't cooperating. So, we'd just hang out at the club or at the Morrisons' until someone drove us home or picked us up. And one of the parents would sail the boat back later."

"So that's what we did today," Bonnie looked wistfully at her cousin. "No funny business, just boating, skiing, telling old stories, eating fried perch, and playing Sheepshead."

"Sheeps-what?" Leah asked.

"Sheepshead," Bonnie said. "It's the Wisconsin state card game, according to Uncle Leo. It's umm, kind of like Euchre."

"Oh, so Jake staying at the cottage isn't doomed?" Leah questioned.

"Not in the least." Bonnie assured her.

"What about his Aunt Evelyn? She was all wound up, ranting and wringing her hands about the youth of today."

"Until she knew what was going on?" Bonnie guessed.

"That was kind of funny, once your Grandma told her you were at the Morrison's, she packed up the kids and headed back before you and Jake were even dropped off."

"Leah, it was so much fun! We actually talked, like, really talked. And you should be thanking me."

Leah paused with a concerned expression, "Why, pray-tell, should I be thanking you?"

""Because, for all those hours we talked," Bonnie explained, "We talked about one thing more than his mother, more all his whining about Marta, the cottage, or even blathering about baseball with the boys. And trust me, that's really saying something. The one thing that boy wanted to talk about: 'you'."

"Shut the front door," Leah said in disbelief. "Bonnie Lee, you better be pulling my leg."

"Swear on the Bible with both hands, the God's-honest truth," Bonnie said. "In case you're wondering, I think you've got the boys' attention."

"Leah sighed, weighing it all out. "So now what do I do for the next four-and-a-half weeks?"

"What us girls always do, sweetheart," Bonnie answered with a sly voice.

"Oh boy," Leah wondered about where this conversation

Chapter Twenty-One

was going. "What's that?"

"Play hard to get," Bonnie and Leah laughed and the two began planning the weekend ahead.

Chapter Twenty-Two
Heart and Soul

"I swear I hear that bell in my sleep," Bonnie undid her bandana as she walked out of the diner.

"You and me both," Leah stopped mid-step and pointed toward the Stanton cottage. "What the heck are they doing?"

There were four men on the roof and ladders thrown up against the side of the cottage. A trailer littered with shingles and trim pieces was squeezed in the side yard and vehicles were strewn around the front and parked in the neighbor's yard.

"Must be a Stanton work day," smirked Bonnie. As they got closer, they could hear Lucy hollering.

"Charlie, are you sure that's gonna fix it?" she yelled.

"Aunt Lucy," Charles looked down, wiping his brow. "May I remind you that I'm the licensed contractor out here?"

"And may I remind you, Charlie, that I was here when they laid the trusses for that roof," she shot back.

Evelyn walked over to try to get her mother to tone it down. "Mom, it looks fine. The boys have been here since seven. The boathouse is completely reshingled, they fixed the concern on the truss, and resheathed the whole north side where the leak was by the exhaust vent. Let them finish the drip edge so we all can go home, please."

"Um, Aunt Evelyn," interjected Jake as he dropped a flat of shingles back onto the trailer. "I thought you were going to show me your list today."

Evelyn shot a look at Lucy, who nodded her head before she answered him. "I guess we could start today." She turned toward the house. "Come with me, Jacob. I have some things I need to explain." As Jake followed her inside, Bonnie and Leah waved to Lucy.

Chapter Twenty-Two

"Hello, girls, done making shakes for the day?"

"Yeah, we thought we'd stop by and see how things were going here," Bonnie pointed toward the roof.

"Oh, they're going okay. I guess I'm good with it," she talked loudly over her shoulder. "And just because I don't have a fancy license doesn't mean I can't tell what looks right."

"Lucy," Alvin gave a short glance, as he steadied the ladder for Ron to reset the trim.

"So what are you girls up to tonight?"

"Well, we were gonna have dinner with Gram and hang with them a little, probably stay the night, as we have first shift tomorrow," Bonnie replied.

"That," Leah added, "And Joe has friends over at the house, playing Madden on the Super Nintendo all night."

"So, what is Jake up to?" asked Leah, not seeing him at the moment.

"Ahh," Lucy glanced toward the cottage, "Jake is gonna be here starting tonight so, you know."

"What's he doing for dinner?" asked Bonnie. "I can check with Gram if he can join us."

"He would probably appreciate that. All that's in the fridge now are some cold cuts and I'm not sure about his cooking skills if he went to the market. That's nice of you girls."

"You're welcome," Bonnie glanced back as the girls headed back towards the farmhouse.

About ninety minutes later, Leah followed Bonnie up the dirt road.

"So, did you call ahead?" asked Leah as they crossed the highway.

"What fun is that? This is a surprise."

She walked up and knocked rapidly on the door.

Silence.

Bonnie knocked again, louder, and then they heard some movement.

"Hello?" came a groggy voice from inside the cottage.

"Hey, Jake, it's Bonnie and me," Leah called through the door. "Thought we'd stop by."

"Oh, hang on," he opened the door in shorts and a still-dirty T-shirt with slept-on hair. "I crashed out after they left. It was a long day, working with the guys."

"I can tell," Bonnie took in his disheveled state. "How would you like chicken pot pie for dinner?"

"That sounds awesome," Jake's stomach growled as he realized how hungry he was. "I'm starving."

"We figured you were," Bonnie and Leah exchanged a humorous glance.

"Let me grab my shoes and clean up real quick and I'll be back down." He headed upstairs and, after about fifteen minutes, the three were walking back to the Beck farmhouse, drawn by the smells drifting from the open windows.

Over dinner, Harold pointed a fork at Jake, "So you-all shingled the house and the boathouse in a day? That's pretty darn good, especially with two foremen running the show."

"We didn't reshingle the whole house, just the side which had the leak. Mainly, I worked with a few of the cousins and we did the boathouse after Uncle Charles showed us what to do. He and the rest of the adults worked on getting the roof done. They spent half the time having to run and get more supplies."

"So, you are out at the cottage now?" Clara looked at the boy.

"Yes, I still need to repaint the boathouse and most of the house. Plus, they want the crawl-space basement and the boathouse cleaned out. I'm sure there is more if I get through that."

"Aunt Clara, this chicken pot pie is amazing," Leah mentioned as she reached for seconds.

"Thank you, dear,"

"Yes, very good. Thank you for asking me over for dinner," Jake looked across to the girls. "So, what are you all planning for the evening?"

"Well, Joe has a slumber party with a bunch of his friends over, so we are gonna stay here tonight and just walk to the diner in the morning," Bonnie answered.

"We were talking about watching a movie," Leah

Chapter Twenty-Two

elbowed her cousin.

"Which movie?" Jake asked.

"Big," Bonnie replied as she elbowed Leah back.

"I love that movie," Clara came back from the kitchen with an empty tupperware container. "And I love me some Tom Hanks."

"Easy there, dear," Harold chuckled at his wife.

"He *is* pretty cute. Have you seen it, Jake?" Leah's eyes crossed to his.

"It's been a while. I'll stay and watch it with you, if you want."

"I'll make up some popcorn," Clara went back into the kitchen. Harold mentioned to Jake he was going to go watch a ballgame upstairs.

"Why's that?" Jake wondered.

"Clara likes her time with Tom to be uninterrupted," Harold said with a laugh as he headed upstairs.

In the living room, the layout was a sofa and loveseat set and a beanbag chair pushed off to the side. Jake, who had spent numerous days here before, was planning on taking his usual seat on the beanbag, but Bonnie was already sitting in it. Jake, a little confused, took a seat on the far end of the sofa, nearer to the beanbag chair and Bonnie. After a few minutes, Leah and Clara came in, carrying bowls of popcorn.

"Wanna share, Farmer Tan?" Leah sat down on the sofa. "It's okay," she scooted just a little closer with the popcorn between them and added, as Georgian as she could, "I don't bite."

Jake gave her an uncertain look and reached for the popcorn.

Soon, they were all engrossed in the movie, enjoying the beautiful story before them.

As the movie finished, Clara stretched from her seat. "Well, ladies and gentleman, I am going to retire, as tomorrow is gonna be a busy enough Sunday," turning off the kitchen lights as she went upstairs. "Make sure you turn down all the lights when you all get back."

"We will, Grandma," said Bonnie as they headed out toward the porch.

As they made their way up the road, back to the cottage, Leah took in the view. The sun was just starting to get lower in the sky and the lake shimmered with a golden hue. "It sure is beautiful," was all she could say.

Bonnie reached for her hand, "Why don't we all go back to the bench and chairs by the dock that look out onto the lake?"

"You want to come in for a minute and help me grab drinks?" asked Jake. Leah was about to, until Bonnie mentioned they could wait a minute.

"If you wouldn't mind bringing them out for us in a basket," she glanced around and there were a lot of families out on their docks enjoying the evening. "The last thing I want to do is make the front page of the community gossip column."

"Good thought," Jake went in and grabbed a 7-Up for Bonnie, a cream soda for himself, and a Diet Coke for Leah, as they didn't have sweet tea. When he joined them down by the dock the girls were already in deep conversation. Jake handed them their drinks and sat down in a chair.

"So, Jake," said Bonnie, "Would you want to be a kid again or skip it and be in your thirties?"

"Gosh, I'd love to skip all the crap and be an adult. Dive right in, you know. I can't wait. And Bonnie, you remember me at that age. I was a mess."

"Yes, you were," Bonnie agreed. "Didn't know what to do with you half the time. Trying so hard to impress the girls, you were a lot like Josh in Big, totally clueless."

"What about you, Leah?" Jake noticed she had gone silent.

"I would love to be twelve again," she whispered after a few moments. Bonnie moved her hand on top of her friend's and squeezed as Leah looked out at the water. Jake saw the change between the girls at this statement and cautiously asked, "Do you mind telling me—"

Before he could finish, Bonnie cut him off. "Jacob," was all she said as she pulled in defensively toward Leah.

Chapter Twenty-Two

"Bonnie," Leah's vision was as unchanging as her voice, "It's okay. I...I can talk about it. I need to talk about it. For me, that movie was about, in a way, memories we have in the past and cherishing them. And my twelfth year, I will cherish for all my life. That was the last year before we really knew..." Her voice went quiet.

Jake looked puzzled at Bonnie, unsure what to ask or if he should. Leah finally glanced at Jake and he could see the life she was reliving behind her eyes. She cleared her throat and turned as she clutched Bonnie's hands within hers.

"It was the year before we knew about the cancer," she began. "We had gone to Ocoee that summer and Mom and I had hiked, just her and I, all the way to Chilhowee. We sat and looked over that valley and she must have told me stories for what seemed like forever, about how our family had come there and how she had grown up crashing around and playing in the curving blue water below us. She was vibrant and full of life and she was so beautiful." Leah slipped her hand into her shirt and pulled out a two-part gold necklace. "That was the year she gave me this."

"Wow, that's really pretty," Jake watched the charm shimmer in the twilight. "What does it say?" Leah unlatched the two chains and held them within her hands as if she was holding priceless china. She clicked them together and then opened the link that conjoined together to make a heart.

"It says, 'Love isn't love till you give it away,'" said Leah as the locket trembled within her hands. "She put this half around my neck that day as we looked out over the valley and we laughed and cried and she promised that she would love me with all her heart 'til her dying breath," she struggled with her next words. "If I only knew...I would have frozen time forever."

"What...what was she like?" asked Jake.

"Confident. And if she was right, well, good luck to you, even if she wasn't," Leah relished in the memory. "And she could lean into a conversation that maybe wasn't quite involving her and make it her own with the grace of a ballerina. Her laugh and, oh, her sense of humor. Now, my mom, mind you, was as straight an arrow as you would ever find and if foul language ever neared my mouth, I'd get it washed out in a heartbeat." Leah shook her head. "But my mom, Miss Second Row in the Choir on Sunday, could drop one out of nowhere that would make a sailor blush and then keep on walking like it was your problem, not hers. She was bold, feisty, passionate."

Leah clutched the locket. "And she was my everything . She loved me so much." She turned to Bonnie. "You know, Bee, I think she almost loved me as much as she loved Pacha."

"Pacha?" asked Jake.

"Her dog," Leah's eyes gleamed. "That dog would get away with murder, but he knew no matter what he did or got into, if he could outrun my dad to the arms of grace, he was safe."

"Anymore, I miss that the most."

"Miss what?" Bonnie asked as she pulled Leah in.

"I miss her arms. She would hold me tight when I was little and I'd struggle with all my might and she'd say in my ear, 'My little river, don't run wild,'" whispered Leah as she looked back at the purple hues of the sunset to try to catch up with her emotions.

"Little river?" asked Jake.

"My middle name is Ocoee. Leah Ocoee Eaton." She got to her feet and looked out at the water talking to herself, as much as to them, "I feel at home here but, then again, I always feel at home by the water. It's a part of me in a way, and it makes me feel a part of my mother is still with me." She turned to Bonnie and they held each other tight.

Jake awkwardly waited until they were at peace. After a few minutes, Bonnie turned back to Jake. "Morning is coming early. We best get back to the house before Gram comes looking for us," she said as the three made their way back to the highway.

Jake pulled Bonnie in for a hug. "Have a good night."

"You, too."

"Night, Leah." Jake wasn't clear on what he should do, as he wasn't sure about a hug, but he didn't want to look stupid with a handshake, so he waved.

Chapter Twenty-Two

"Night, Farmer Tan." Leah shook her head as she and Bonnie walked back up the road to the farmhouse. Jake went back to the front porch of the cottage and watched until he saw Beck's porch light turn out before going inside.

He was about to grab another cream soda from the fridge, but something on the marble counter caught his eye. The red light on the answering machine was flashing by the phone. Jake hit play and his stomach sank as the voice crackled on the recording.

"Hey, Jake, it's Dad. We should talk. Grab a pen. My phone number for my hotel room is..." Jake stopped the recording, grabbed a pen, and replayed the message as he sat on a stool in the dark.

Chapter Twenty-Three
Father Figure

Jake looked at the number written on the piece of paper, took a sip of the cream soda and braced himself for the conversation he had hoped to avoid as he began punching in the numbers for the calling card into the phone.

After an initial click, there were two buzzes on the line.

"Good evening, Hyatt Regency Dearborn, how can I help you?" came a woman's warm voice over the phone.

"Yes, could I have room 520, please? Paul Stanton."

"Yes, sir, may I let him know who is calling?" she asked.

"Yes, please tell him that it's Jacob Stanton."

"Thank you, Jacob. Hold, please." There was a pause and the sounds of Motown came over the line.

"Thank you for holding," the receptionist came back. "I'll send your call up now."

Buzz, buzz. "Hello," came Paul's voice.

"Hey, Dad, I got your message."

"Yes, thanks for calling me back. Your grandmother said she let you stay out at the cottage tonight. I figured you'd be in when I called earlier," Paul quizzed his son.

"Mrs. Beck invited me over for dinner, as I've not gone shopping yet, so I stayed and watched a movie because Bonnie and her cousin were there," Jake carefully chose his words.

"I'm sure you did," Paul knew his son all-too-well. "So, how'd you talk my mom into letting you stay out at the cottage already?"

"I made a deal with Grandpa. He said if I kept my half, he would take care of it with Grandma and Aunt Evelyn."

"Really? That is some serious negotiation on your grandpa's part," Paul's curiosity piqued as to what his son was

Chapter Twenty-Three

on the hook for. "What did you have to promise in that bargain?"

"I have to get a bunch of work done on the cabin. It's a pretty long list," Jake sighed.

Paul chuckled. "That sounds like Dad. And?" He waited.

"The second part, he said that every Thursday he wants me to spend the whole day with Aunt Edith for whatever she needs."

"And that," Paul slapped his knee as he laughed, "Is why you're there. Your grandmother and all the ladies each have days of the week they go and help Edith at the manor, take her out for the day to run errands, go see family, et cetera. Thursday is your grandmother's day. Since those two have power-struggled for decades, Edith will take your grandmother all over God's green earth and often makes sure to save visits to parts of the family who may not be on the best terms with your grandmother for those Thursdays."

"So, while you are there, your grandfather got you to take your grandmother's spot for a month, which I'm sure he took full credit for and, in return, he sealed you getting to stay at the cottage. Pretty sharp of the old man, I must say," Paul smiled to himself. "So, how's that going? You getting along well with Edith?"

"Dad, Aunt Edith is awesome," exclaimed Jake. "She's got some wild stories."

Paul laughed. "You haven't heard half of them. There are stories I was told by my great uncles about the wild littlest Glass sister that test credibility but are probably true. I am glad you're getting along with her. Speaking of getting along..." He let out a long breath. "I talked with your mother Thursday night and—"

"Dad, I—" Jake tried to explain and Paul's tone changed.

"Don't interrupt me," Paul's voice cutting him off. "I know you don't want to go to Stanford. Anyone within earshot of you for more than five minutes hears your bleeding-heart sob story of how unfair your life is. But here's the thing, son. Your mom and I want you to at least look at it. It's a good school and she has put in the effort far beyond what I feel you deserve to make that still be possible. I know you two rarely see eye-to-

Father Figure

eye and seem to draw swords after three words about anything. Which is part of why I signed off on the trip this summer, to hopefully give you two some space and myself some peace." Paul tried to relax his emotions. "Yet, here's what blows my mind. Before you left, you were asked by me, not just your mother, to do one thing. Do you remember what I asked?" Paul waited for a reply.

"That I call Mr. Carroll," said Jake quietly.

"Yes, to call the man. Then go and do a lunch interview that your mother prepped the questions for. All you had to do was show up at Ventana Canyon, eat a nice lunch that I'd prepaid for, and give halfway coherent answers to questions served on a tee. I hope standing up an attorney I have to work with next month so as not to affect your social life was worth it," Paul stated before further narrowing the tone so Jake could clearly understand him.

"I know I have been on the road a lot. Hell, I'm in Detroit right now, dealing with another exporter trying to pull a fast one. And I didn't personally hold your hand and walk you to the meeting. But, may I remind you of what you said to your mother the other night? 'You are eighteen in two months. You are an adult.' If that is truly the case, son, show me you can act like one."

Jake knew his father was right. "I'm sorry, Dad, it's just I—"

"Stop it," Paul interrupted him. He paced for a minute in his room, letting his voice relax a little. "Jake, no excuses, I don't want to hear them. This was something easy and you blew it off. Plain and simple. So, what are you going to do about it?"

"What do you mean?"

Paul took a few deep breaths, exhaled, then spoke. "You need to call Mr. Carroll and apologize and reschedule for when we get back in late July. That is non-negotiable. And I want you to call your mother tonight, as well. I'm calling her in an hour, so I'll know."

"Okay, I'll call Mom,"
"Good."
"Oh, Dad, about Mr. Carroll's number..." Jake started to

Chapter Twenty-Three

get out his pen and paper.

"Actually, Jake, I'm going to give it to you myself," Paul let satisfaction creep into his voice.

"How are you doing that?" came Jake's confused answer.

"When I see you on Tuesday in Chicago."

"What?" Jake nearly dropped the phone.

"You, me, Grandpa, Uncle Bobby, and Jenny are going to a Cubs game Tuesday afternoon. I switched up my flights. I'm flying into Chicago for the day before heading home. Bobby is picking me up at the airport and you and Grandpa will meet us at Bobby's. We have a client who has season tickets, pretty good seats from what I hear. Six tickets are waiting for me at will-call. So, because I'm feeling nice, you can bring a friend. From the gossip I've heard, you currently have... two?" he questioned. "I guess you can pick which one. I swear, son, with all the trouble that got stirred up with Marta this spring, I figured you would take a break."

Jake blushed through the phone. "I'll ask."

"Perfect," Paul's voice warmed as he thought of all that the last few years had brought. "Son, I love you and your mother does, too. I know you feel she doesn't show that with clarity sometimes, but that's just how she was raised. But she really does want the best for you and for you not to struggle like we did in our early years."

"I know," said Jake. "It's just..." He wondered if he wanted to touch on it.

"Just that you two are a lot alike. Two very passionate souls. You just need to learn when, in your passion, which battles to pick," Paul laughed. "I'm going to review my contract notes before I talk with your mom in an hour. Have a good night at the cottage. I love you, Jacob."

"I love you too, Dad."

"See you Tuesday, son. Good night."

"Night, see you Tuesday." Jake hung up the phone. In the dark, he collected the many thoughts crashing through his brain, and got out his calling card to call his mother.

Chapter Twenty-Four
Smells Like Teen Spirit

"Bonnie, that fish is looking at me. Are you really going to eat that?" Leah looked away and tried to focus on her spinach omelet.

"Not up for pickled herring, cuz?" Bonnie moved the fish toward her cousin with her fork. "It's a Swedish thing."

"That's cool for you but, I'm just saying, we eat fish in Georgia, but it ain't at breakfast, normally deep-fried, and not staring at me," Leah turned her chair so she could look at something else. She glanced at the three empty chairs across from her. "Did the boys really go back up again?"

"Are you kidding?" Bonnie looked toward the buffet tables. "Dylan, Jake, and Ronnie will eat until they can't move. That's what they..." her voice choked. "Oh, dear god."

"What?" Krissy looked up from her L.J. Smith novel.

"Mote's here," Bonnie uneasily alerted them.

"Well, this is gonna get interesting," Krissy went back to the world of Elena Gilbert.

"Interesting how?" Leah looked over her shoulder toward the loud laughs and back-slapping camaraderie coming from the opposite end of the dining hall. Her eyes stopped on a boy with wildly unkempt red hair who was wearing a Beastie Boys T-shirt and bright orange Jams.

"His name is Moat?" asked Leah.

Krissy rolled her bright green eyes as she explained, "That is Montegue Teague or Mote as he's been called since they screwed up his name in third grade."

"What happened?" Leah was intrigued.

"He always went by Mo, per his parents' request so he could pass Kindergarten – cause what kids gonna ever spell that

Chapter Twenty-Four

right – and it said his first name, his nickname, and last name on the paperwork. The receptionist typed it in wrong and printed 'MoTe Ague' by accident on everything that year. So, it stuck."

"So, is he a bad boy?" Leah shot Krissy a mischievous grin.

"No," disgust filled Bonnie's voice, "He's an idiot boy and, to those morons over there, he is a god."

Krissy flipped her blonde locks as she turned to Leah. "You know they always say look before you leap. Mote's life motto is "Leap and then look to make sure you see everyone's reaction as you nearly maim yourself."

"Oh," Leah took in the advice while watching the boy. "At least it won't be a dull afternoon."

"Sweetheart, just be careful what that loon tries to talk you into," Krissy warned. "He's a fast sweet-talker and you don't know you're going over the cliff until he tells you to wave."

"So, the type of boy my Grandma would 'bless his heart'?"

"Yes," Krissy and Bonnie replied in unison.

"Here they come," Bonnie busied herself with her herring.

"Top o' the morning. If it ain't my Bonnie lass," Mote greeted with a little Irish brogue in his voice. "How are you, my dear? And bless me, who is this cailín álainn?"

"This is my cousin. Mote, please behave," Bonnie, taking a defensive stance before Leah decided to have a little fun.

Leaning into her high-southern dialect, Leah looked at the boy with her best Scarlett O'Hara impression. "Your reputation precedes you, good sir. You're a real, live, outlaw, aren't you?"

A twinkle rolled in Mote's eyes. "Well, I may be the outlaw, darling, but you're the one stealing my heart."

"Oh my god, I love that movie, how many times have you seen it?" Leah was intrigued.

"My older sister is obsessed with it. Probably thirty on the VHS," Mote placed his palms down and leaned in. "You?"

"I worked at a theater the summer it came out. I watched it so much I could mouth the lines of Geena," said Leah.

Smells Like Teen Spirit

"That's awesome and you rock!" He turned and yelled to boys with his arms up in a 'V', "This Southern belle can go line-for-line on Thelma and Louise. We gotta throw out all the stops today!"

From the far end of the hall, a lady with red hair and a blue Bollman hat caught his attention and said, "Montegue, either eat your breakfast in peace or eat it outside."

With renewed courtesy Mote replied, "Yes, Mum," as he took a seat next to Krissy, directly opposite Leah. "Okay, Miss Silver Screen, best underrated movie you saw last year."

"The Fisher King, what's yours?"

Mote looked across at Leah as if he was beholding a unicorn. With a wonderment that left him speechless. "The Fisher King was beautiful."

Leah then broke into character. *"How can you find that which my brightest and bravest could not?"*

And Mote continued with the polish of a Shakespearean actor in a hushed tone, *"And the fool replied, 'I don't know. I only knew that you were thirsty.'"* They held a silent reverence to the scene.

Krissy, lost as to what they were talking about, finally said, "I think my grandma saw Dances with Wolves. Why are you thirsty?" she asked, confused.

"Don't worry about it, sweetheart," Dylan slid in next to her with two plates mounded high with food.

"Did you get me a lemon tart?" she inquired, forgetting the film critics at the table.

"Yes, it's under the second plate with the pancakes," Dylan lifted a pancake as he began to shovel them into his mouth.

"Oh, umm, thank you," Krissy said with resignation as she viewed the squashed tart.

When Ronnie and Jake sat, Mote turned to Leah, "We shall continue our intriguing conversation later, my lady."

He broke into a stiff and stately pose and turned to the boys pointing a fork with a presence that would impress Churchill himself, "So men, life is either a daring adventure or nothing at all. What does today bring?"

Chapter Twenty-Four

Dylan looked at his crazed friend, "Buoy racing, if your junkers had a tune-up."

"My Kawasaki will dust your ass any day, Morrison," Mote rose to the challenge.

"So, what are the rules for buoy racing?" Leah wondered.

"There are two ways to do it. There is the relay, where you have a team race, one lap each rider, fastest time wins. Or a single-rider, full-lake buoy race for the fastest time. We will need a judge by the buoys and a judge by the dock to keep time and the finish." Dylan explained using salt and pepper shakers to show the format.

"Hey Krissy," asked Bonnie, "Is your brother's Ski-Doo running okay?"

"Yeah, why?" asked Krissy.

"I want to race today," Bonnie pointed at Mote.

"Doth the lady challenge us to a speed race?" Mote's eyes were grinning.

"The lady doth."

"Okay, we will need two boats out by the buoys to confirm points and a timekeeper and the racers are Mote, myself, Bonnie." Dylan was counting out the racers and roles.

"And me!" said Krissy raising her hand

"Really, sweetheart?" Dylan spoke before his mind could catch his mouth.

"Well, why not," she said, now staring with eyes of fire at her boyfriend. "Us girls wanna have fun too, right, Bonnie?"

"Yeah, you betcha."

Mote looked at Leah, "And would you mind, my lady, keeping time?"

"I would be happy to."

"Meeting point and start will be at my grandpa's dock," Dylan informed the group. "Ronnie, can you set up out by the east channel, and Jake, if you can, be in the Landon's boat out by the buoy in the south bay?"

"Sure, man, we're on it," Jake high-fived Ronnie.

Brunch adjourned and the preparations began.

At 2:00 pm, Mote pulled up to Morrison's dock on a

neon-orange-trimmed Kawasaki. Krissy and Bonnie arrived shortly after, with Leah and Bonnie on the blue Ski-Doo and Krissy on her pink Yamaha SuperJet.

Dylan was wiping down his red Sea-Doo and looked out at the buoys to confirm Jake and Ronnie were in position.

"Okay," he cleared his throat. "The rules: the race will begin with a call for all racers to start the engines, followed by a countdown of five and a yell to go, which starts the time," he pointed out across the lake. "The race course will start with the racers rounding the south buoy, then rounding the east buoy and tracking the north outer shore path 'til passing Landon's pier with the crossing return to the dock. The first to step on dry ground, confirmed by Leah, will be declared the winner. The path must be kept. Not fully making a complete circle of the buoy adds one minute to the final time. The official winner will be declared after Ronnie and Jake return and confirm no penalties. All agree to the tenets of the race?" asked Dylan.

"Yes," Mote, Krissy, and Bonnie all gave a thumbs up.

"Okay, Jake and Ronnie are in position," Dylan looked out at the boats. He handed Leah his Michael Jordan stopwatch, "To your crafts, racers."

As Krissy and Bonnie settled onto their jet skis, Mote and Dylan glared at each other.

"Any side bets, Teague?" Dylan stared dead-eyed at Mote.

"What are you wagering, Morrison?" Mote returned the cold stare.

"The loser between you two has to shut their yap for the rest of the day," Bonnie overrode both of them.

Krissy added, "And if Bonnie or I win, you both do." She high-fived Bonnie.

"Dream on, blondie," Dylan laughed with Mote.

"Watch yourself, or that cold front moving in may arrive early," her cold tone matching the look she gave her boyfriend. .

"OOOHH," Mote howled. "May the best gentleman or lady win."

Leah cleared her voice. "Racers in position." She waited

Chapter Twenty-Four

for all to make sure they were cleared and ready. "Racers, start your engines," she said to the sound of the rumble and chugging sound of the jet skis. "On your marks, get set...Five, four, three, two, one...GO!" she shouted.

And they were off, rapid blurs streaming across the lake. Dylan and Mote were neck-and-neck, with Bonnie close behind and Krissy taking a slightly off-to-the-outside path which, to the initial observer, made no sense until Bonnie saw the issue.

Dylan and Mote were rocking against each other's chop and Krissy had a cleaner ride toward the first buoy and began to swing south to a counterclockwise rounding of the buoy. They made a clean pass just as they neared and created a counter wave that rocked Mote enough to make him throttle down to avoid washing his motor and stalling. Dylan tried to break against the chop, but also had to slow, and Krissy rocked out toward the second buoy seconds ahead of Mote, with Dylan fast on their heels and Bonnie close behind.

As they approached the second buoy near the channel, Jake watched as Dylan tried to outsmart his girl by using her maneuver, but forgot the shallow water and had to veer sharply to avoid grounding out, forcing him to backtrack as Mote whizzed by. Krissy turned and headed toward the north shore path, full-speed toward her pier. Her dad sat on the dock, cheering his daughter to victory.

Dylan's jet ski may have had the most horsepower, but its size was becoming a disadvantage; he had botched and lost time on both buoys. Mote was slowly gaining on Krissy since his engine had the horsepower for the straightaway. As they neared the dock, Krissy began to prepare for her turn when she saw a water skier coming up from the west end of the lake, by the lodge. She knew if she risked a full gun to the slip just behind the boat, she would lose a few initial seconds, but Mote, in a straight cross, would be hitting full wake on his shorter path from the large motor of the speedboat and would probably slow his time.

Krissy opened full throttle and raced toward the angle of coming just behind the speedboat exiting the no-wake zone before gunning it into open water.

Mote saw her head at an off-angle and laughed to himself as he sped closer to her, and his turn. It was then that he heard the roar of the giant powerboat. He turned and she slipped gracefully behind them at a safe distance. Mote looked at the giant waves now rolling ahead of him. His skills let him ride high on the troughs but, by the time he cleared it, Krissy was at full-throttle from her angled path toward the Morrison dock. It was going to be a photo finish as their boats screamed across the water.

Minutes later, they both neared the shore, skimming into the shallow water, the racers leaped from their crafts and dashed the final steps to the shore. Sadly, Mote was no match for the Wisconsin regionals track star as she cut through the water with grace and leaped onto the beach, arms in the air, and shouted, "Girls rule!" while Mote stood knee-deep in the water, hearing Dylan pull up alongside him.

"When do you think she'll stop talking about this?" asked Mote under his breath.

"I'm hoping sometime before I die," Dylan watched as Krissy bum-rushed Leah, who joined her in her victory dance. Bonnie pulled her jetski alongside the dock, clambered up, and into the jubilant arms of her friends as they chanted and yelled, "Girls rule, girls rule!."

"So," Mote glanced at Dylan, "Up for a game of Sheepshead?"

Chapter Twenty-Five
Man on the Moon

Bonnie sat back in the lounge chair next to Leah on the screened-in porch. Jake was flipping burgers and brats on the outside grill.

"So, is there beer in them? That just sounds gross," Leah gave a cringing look to Bonnie while Jake managed the charcoal grill outside.

"No, you simmer them in beer with onions and butter and then you put them on the grill. That's why Jake brought the kitchen pot outside," explained Bonnie.

"So, this is another Wisconsin thing?"

"Yup. They've been making beer brats in Wisconsin since the twenties," Bonnie called down. "Hey, Jake!"

"What, Bonnie?" Jake looked up as he fought with a flame that was trying to turn a burger into a piece of charcoal.

"Remember, I like mine a soft medium, right?"

"Sure, whatever you want, *Your Highness*," was Jake's sarcastic reply.

"Should I tell him I just want one that's not a hockey puck?" Leah watched the flames leap from the grill.

"That works," Bonnie laughed. "So, are they about done, Jake?"

"Pretty close. If you two wouldn't mind setting the table, we should be ready here in a minute."

"Sounds good," Bonnie and Leah got up and headed into the house.

They were soon seated at the table with brats, burgers, some coleslaw, and German potato salad that Bonnie had brought over. Jake opened his bag of Tato Wilds Tato Skins.

Bonnie looked at the bag with skepticism, "Where did

you even get those?"

"Mote gave me an extra bag to take back after lunch this afternoon at the Morrison's."

Bonnie peered into the bag. "If that was your point of recommendation, I'm not sure."

"I'll try one," Leah grabbed a handful of oval crisps. "That Mote dude is full of surprises."

"Yes and, thankfully, none of them exploded today," Bonnie recalled. "Jake, do you remember when he tried to make that firework and nearly blew his hand off?"

"Yes," Jake remembered back to that wild day, where the ball of fire left a four-foot crater on the beach. "He was, what, fourteen?"

"His mom seemed nice," Leah noted.

"Oh, Mrs. Teague is a refined and proper woman and God blessed her with Mote for a son." Bonnie continued with several more Mote stories.

"Well, bless his heart," Leah held her hand to her chest mockingly as they all laughed.

"So, Jake, what's the plan for this week?" Leah asked as they cleared the table.

"Tomorrow, I probably need to get some painting done and Gram wants me to be in town tomorrow evening," he replied.

"Why's that?" Bonnie cocked an eye. "Does this have to do with the call with your mom and dad?"

"Yeah," answered Jake

"How did that go, anyway?" Leah saw the concern brewing on his face.

"Dad basically chewed me out for not taking care of the interview before I left and how it got Mom all wound up and pissed off. So I apologized and told him I'd do the interview and after that fun conversation, I called my mom," Jake complained.

"Wow, out of the frying pan straight into the fire," Leah whistled.

"You ain't kidding," Jake nodded. "It was actually pretty civil. She wanted an apology for messing up things with the lawyer. I mean, how was I supposed to know that they had a

Chapter Twenty-Five

business deal with the guy? I told her I was sorry and that I was going to call him," said Jake. "And you won't believe what she did."

"What?" asked Bonnie. "Demand you home on the next flight?"

"Actually, she apologized for some of what she said the other night."

Bonnie showed her surprise. "That doesn't happen often. That's a good development."

"I mean, she knows she has a temper, and she says I seem to know the shortest path to find it," Jake looked at Bonnie and she rolled her eyes.

"When are you gonna learn to not hack off to your mom, dude," Leah teased.

"I wish. That's a minefield I never seem to survive crossing."

"So, what's the end result?" asked Bonnie.

"My dad is going to deliver the number of the guy for me to call in person."

"What, your dad is flying up here just to give you a phone number?" Leah was totally confused.

"No," said Jake. "My dad has been in Detroit on business and instead of flying straight home, he is flying into Chicago on Tuesday morning. My grandpa and I are meeting him at Uncle Bobby's because we are all going to a Cubs game."

"Oh my God, I love the Cubs! I've seen them play in Atlanta," interjected Leah.

"It is pretty cool," said Jake. "About that—"

"About what?" Bonnie wondered where this was going.

"My dad has one extra ticket. He said I could bring a friend."

"Really, a friend?" Bonnie made air quotes.

"I'll be your *friend*, Farmer Tan, if I get to see a Cubs game," Leah, grinning, glanced at her cousin. "You don't mind, do you, Bonnie?"

"I'm scheduled for Tuesday, anyway," Bonnie gave a resigned reply. "You all have fun." She turned to Leah and added, "It'll give you a chance to meet the Stantons; they're an interesting group of folks."

"My grandpa is pretty cool, and Uncle Bobby is hysterical," Jake tried to improve on her comment. "I guess Jenny is coming, too."

"Really?" Bonnie warmed up for a minute. "That kid is so cute."

"If you're good going, Leah…and Bonnie, you're good with not going, I guess this is all set. I can have us swing by the house on the way out of town."

"Sounds like a plan, Farmer Tan. I can't believe I'm going to Wrigley Field," Leah said before asking her cousin, "You ever been, Bonnie?"

"I caught a game about a year ago when I was down visiting Raff," she replied quietly

"Wait, is this that sailor-boy you told me about?"

"Leah, stop," Bonnie gave a warning in her voice.

Bonnie tried not to let her emotions get ahead of her. "Besides, it doesn't really matter now. I haven't heard from him in over six weeks and from where he may get sent next, I may not see him for years. So there's not much to say," she got quiet.

Jake changed the subject to something less sensitive. "So, I'll see you Tuesday morning, Leah. I'll call you girls tomorrow night."

"Okay, sounds good," said Leah as she and Bonnie started to pack things up to head back to her house.

"Well, good night," said Jake as they walked to the door

"Good night, Jake," said Bonnie

"Good night, Farmer Tan," said Leah

On the drive home, Bonnie was quiet. "You okay there?" said Leah. "Are you upset that I'm going with Jake and not you? I thought you were okay with that now?"

"It's just, I wish I could go back to Chicago and Raff would be there. I'm tired of my heart getting pulled one way and then being left behind, Leah."

As they were unloading the car, Bonnie's dad met them outside. "Hey girls, hope you had a fun couple days at the lake."

Chapter Twenty-Five

"We did, Dad. How was yours here?" Bonnie asked.

"Not too bad. Got the yard mowed and worked on the garage with your mom. Oh, and Leah, I talked with your dad this afternoon."

Leah stopped, worried where this was going. "How's he doing? Everything okay?"

"He's fine. Sounds like things are coming together in Houston," he tried to be positive, missing the pained look on Leah's face.

"That's good, I guess," she looked away.

"He asked that you give him a call when you got back. He wants to talk with you about some things," Trevor added

"I'm sure he does," was Leah's sour response.

"If you want, you can call him back from the office. That way, you'll have some privacy," Trevor suggested after noticing the tone.

"Thank you," Leah said as she went into the house and grabbed a cup of tea before going to call her father in Houston.

Chapter Twenty-Six
With or Without You

Leah settled down into the executive chair in the office, just off the living room. She relaxed and tried to frame her mind for the questions she wanted answered. She dialed the number to her grandma's house and waited. On the third ring, the weathered drawl of her grandmother came through the phone.

"Hello."

"Good evening, Grandma, it's Leah."

"Oh hi, dear, how are you?" asked Ethel. "Enjoying your time up there? I hope you are having fun with your cousin."

"Bonnie and I are doing all right, been busy hanging out with friends and spending time over at the diner with her family."

"I'm sure. I met Clara before, a long time ago. Glad to hear they are doing well."

"They sure are. Is Dad there?"

"He's here. Hang on, sweetheart. I love you."

"Thanks, Grandma. Love you, too," Leah replied as she heard the phone transfer to her father.

"Hey, honey, how's it going?" Brett asked.

"It's going okay, Dad."

"I tried to call earlier and ended up talking to Trevor for a bit. He said you girls have practically been living out at the lake."

"We stayed out with Clara and helped her at the diner and met up with Bonnie's friends. How are things there?"

"I've been busy checking out the job. There is definitely some potential here. Just trying to decide when and where for the logistics of it."

"Dad, are we talking privately?"

"Yes, I'm in the guest bedroom."

They Say It's a River

Chapter Twenty-Six

"Okay, then give me the real scoop. What's going on?" concern marked her words

"Like I said before you left, the move is going to happen. We are selling the house and moving to Texas," her father reiterated.

"I know, Dad, but I, I don't wanna go."

"I know you are fearful about it, but your whole world isn't going to disappear. It's going to be okay. Don't go looking for trouble that hasn't happened yet," Brett tried to convince her to calm her fears.

"I know, Dad, but I do have one big request. If you do this, I won't fight you as much on the move."

"Oh, boy," Brett wondered, preparing for what pound of flesh she was going to ask for. "What is this request?"

"I don't want to live in Tomball," was Leah's cold reply.

"What?!" he exclaimed, knowing the fireworks this would start.

"Dad, I turn eighteen in six months and then I can go where I want. I don't want to live under Aunt Caroline's thumb. You said the office was near Baytown. I remember we looked at a brochure about how nice it was. Can we look there? Please." Leah leaned into a younger voice

"Honey, we won't be living with Aunt Caroline," Brett answered back, a little defensive.

"Dad, I don't want to live in the same district as her kids. I'm a senior and I have a car. Her oldest can't drive yet. I don't want to be her default driver, sitter, and whatever else she has on her list. I don't think that's asking too much."

"You know your aunt's gonna flip over that," Brett pushed back. "She has it all planned—"

"And that's the problem," she interrupted. "That right there. That's why I don't want to go. And if you want to make sure I leave as soon as I can, go ahead and move us there."

"Leah," Brett snapped, getting irritated with her tone.

"This isn't Aunt Caroline's life, Dad, it's mine!" she shouted before catching herself. "You're making me give up my senior year with all my friends and move to Texas and leave all the family I've ever known, just to pigeonhole me into a world I didn't ask for," she took a breath as she noticed the silence on the other end of the line.

"All I'm asking for is a place within it to call my own. Nothing more. If you want me to go all-in with you, I need to know that you're all-in with me. Okay, Dad?" she pleaded in as calm a tone as she could find.

"Alright, I hear you," Brett gave in after a minute. "I'll look at Baytown."

"Thank you, Dad. I appreciate you hearing me out."

"This isn't easy for either of us." He was tired of beating this topic to death and changed the subject. "So, how are things there? Clara's not working you all too much, is she?"

"No, Daddy, no problem there."

"What have you been up to? Your aunt mentioned a boy," Brett was curious what she'd tell him.

Leah thought through her words so as not to get her father overexcited. "Yes, there is a boy. His name is Jake. He's a close friend of the family that Bonnie's grown up with. His grandparents have a cottage at the lake."

"Really? Well, that's interesting. You all are hanging out there a lot?"

Like a seasoned pro, Leah eyed the question and knew exactly how to field it. "Yes, we had a nice family lunch there the other day." She let that rest a minute before getting to the bigger item at hand, "He invited me to go to a Cubs game Tuesday with his family."

"He invited you to a Cubs game with his family? So, like, a date?" his dad-antenna went up.

"Daddy, relax, just a baseball game. I'm riding down with his grandpa and meeting up with his dad and uncle. It will be fun," Leah continued to downplay it.

"Why isn't he taking Bonnie?"

"Bonnie has to work and I love the Cubs, so win-win," she tried to talk baseball, not Jake.

"I'm not sold, but have fun and try not to get into any trouble."

Chapter Twenty-Six

"Come on, Dad, don't worry, it's me," she joked with him a little.

"It is you and that's why I worry. It's part of the job, sweetie."

"It will be fine."

"Call me Tuesday night when you get back, please, okay?"

"I will. I love you, Dad."

"I love you, too, Leah. Good night."

"Good night," Leah hung up the phone.

She went upstairs to find Bonnie sitting on her bed, looking through a box of notes and pictures. Bonnie had a sad expression on her face as she sifted through the papers.

"You okay there, cuz?" asked Leah.

"I'm fine." But her bloodshot eyes told a far deeper story.

"Reading your letters from that sailor boy?"

"It's been over a month since his last letter. He told me they are safe, but with all the news about fighting and bombings in Europe and Africa, I just worry. I always ask what he's doing, but he never really says. And I miss him so much."

"Where's he at?" asked Leah.

"Somewhere in the Mediterranean. In the last box I sent, I included a new mixtape and I told him how much I loved him and how I wished he could come home."

"When do you think he'll be back?"

"I don't know. He's trying to come back and be stationed out of the Great Lakes in Chicago, but he keeps saying he may get told to stay there and be part of support operations with NATO. If that happens, I won't see him for two years or more. And I don't know if my heart will be able to take it. I always try to have hope but, right now, it's wearing out." She caressed the picture of the two of them at Navy Pier, her heart aching from the uncertainty. "The person I wanted so badly to love me didn't, and the person who loves me with all their heart is worlds apart," she wiped her eyes and longed for what she felt she would never have.

Chapter Twenty-Seven
From a Distance

It was stuffy inside the barracks. The heat of the day still hung in the air. Raff made his way to his bunk assigned for his days ashore.

The mattress wasn't the BeautyRest back home, but it wasn't moving with the waves either. Raff dug through his olive-colored seabag until he found the weathered notepad and his walkman. He adjusted his headphones and pressed play, taking a moment to look at the small plastic picture frame inside the notebook. His heart was a mix of emotions. The smiling girl in her cream-colored beret, with eyes that he longed to see with his own. He held it to his heart before setting it back and grabbing the pen to write.

15 June, 1992

To: Bonnie Cloud
4715 Meadow Ln
Waukesha, WI 53072

From: RSC Raffael Rossi
USS Nitze
Unit 100514, Box 1
FPO AP 96667
Sigonella, Sicily

My dearest B,
I miss you more each day. This wash, rinse, repeat life

Chapter Twenty-Seven

seems to blur into one long day. We are ashore for a few days in Sicily, as of this writing, and it may be some time after this before I am ashore again. It's so beautiful here. I included a picture looking out over the bay. The water in the Mediterranean is so blue, I can't even find the words to describe it.

Someday, I'm going to take you here, if I ever get to call you Mrs. Bonnie Rossi. There is a volcano that perpetually has smoke coming out of the top. I have to admit, it's pretty unnerving, but the locals don't seem to notice.

It is nice to be on dry ground for a few days. It's hard to explain what walking on land feels like after weeks at sea. There are so many amazing things I have seen, like the Rock of Gibraltar, when we first got here, was insane—how big it is and how it's just out there over nothing.

I'm not sure if you've read the news or not, but I may be here longer unless I get approved for the MOS I've put in for. But, remember Sarajevo from the Olympics? Things have gone south there in a big way.

We've been working with a bunch of different units from NATO the last few months. I've met a bunch of cool guys from Britain, Germany, and Italy. This one guy, Antonio, has the last name Rossi, too. But his family isn't from Chicago, they're all from Umbria.

We are all working together, as there has been a lot of fighting going on and people getting run out of their homes and many have died and the brass are talking like it's gonna get a lot worse.

When we ship out, we are going back that way and all communication is gonna be locked down for whatever we are doing next. So, please don't think I'm forgetting you by not writing. But it's a good thing we are doing, Bonnie.

The things I've seen and the even more horrific things I've read in the reports are just awful. The way people treat each other, the cruelty, especially towards women and children, is heartbreaking. We were told we can share that we're delivering medical supplies and food to help them.

Several of us volunteered at a refugee camp a few weeks

From a Distance

ago. There were men, women, and countless children - injured, blinded, starving - most just wanting to find their parents, asking if there was anything we could do. It was there, on my second trip back, that I met Arma and her daughter Emela.

We were handing out clothes and supplies when this little girl in the crowd saw me and ran away like she'd seen a ghost. A little later, she returned and dragged her mother towards me. The mother looked at me, deeply disturbed, and tried to leave, but Emela was determined to reach me. Antonio pointed us to a sitting area with a friend who could translate.

Arma sat there, holding her five-year-old daughter, who wriggled until she broke free and crawled into my lap, giving me a hug. I hugged the little girl back and as she looked at the mother and said "Kao tata". I asked what she was saying. Antonio, with his friend translating quietly now, said, "You remind her of her father." I looked at Arma and began to ask about the father, but the interpreter leaned in and discreetly asked the question himself.

Tears began to roll down Arma's face. "He was shot dead along with others who tried to protect those fleeing the village. Emela knows her father is gone."

It broke my heart, Bonnie. I held Emela as she looked up at me, smiled, and said "nedostaješ mi" (I miss you), then kissed my cheek. Her mother said it was the first time Emela had smiled since they escaped their village.

After a few more minutes, Emela returned to her mother. They both hugged me and Antonio and Arma thanked me for my kindness towards her daughter.

As we prepared to go, I turned to the interpreter and said, "Tell her I pray she finds refuge for them both. She has a beautiful daughter with a truly lovely name, Emela. I'll never forget it."

The woman smiled and said, "Thank you. It's beautiful because it means 'hope'."

Bonnie, when I returned that night to the base, I wept past the tears I could cry. The nights are so long and, often, with the constant change and station, I feel so alone in this

Chapter Twenty-Seven

darkened world.

 When I lie awake at night and all I can hear are the dull sounds of the ship and aircraft, I think of you. As the waves rock me to sleep, I dream of the days when you will be beside me as we rock to sleep and I can hold you 'til the morning.

 There are so many words I wish I could have said to you when I was able to spend those few days last summer - that final look at you as you waved from the gate, and your beret and curls fading into the distance.

 I keep your picture with me inside my pocket above my heart, so that you know you are always close to it. I close my eyes at night and listen to the tape you made me. The last song by Journey, I listen to the most.

 I love you and miss you so much it hurts and know I will always be forever yours, faithfully.

 With all my heart,
 Love,
 Raff

Raff sat quietly, listening to the song's final notes fade as the tape clicked to a stop and he wished he could erase the deep ache within. Wiping his eyes, he folded the letter, gave it a kiss, and tucked it into the envelope as he got ready to sleep.

Chapter Twenty-Eight
Nothing Else Matters

The Buick chugged down Highway 94 as Alvin called over his shoulder, "Getting enough air back there, Jake?" to his grandson in the back seat.

"I'm good, Grandpa." Jake sat with his legs stretched across the back seat.

"Do you have enough legroom? We can switch when we stop for gas," Leah felt bad that Jake was cramped in the back.

"Jake's just fine, Leah," Alvin assured her. "Besides, a lady should sit up front. Right, Jake?"

"Right, Grandpa," Jake chimed in without missing a beat.

"You are so sweet, Mr. Stanton," Leah glanced across to the man in his late sixties wearing a grin that was almost as cockeyed as his Brewers cap.

"Years of practice. If you ask Lucy, she'd tell you I'm still practicing. How are you enjoying the Midwest? A little cooler than Atlanta?"

"Oh, it's very nice, the humidity there this time of year, in the city, is so thick it just slaps you when you go outside."

Alvin chuckled. "You, young lady, are a gas. I hope my grandson back there has some useful conversation today. But not to worry, while Jake is getting his ass handed to him by his father, you, me, Bobby, and Jenny can enjoy the ballgame."

"Thanks," Jake commiserated from the back seat.

"Don't complain to me, you're the one who got yourself into this," Alvin shook his head at his grandson before turning back to Leah. "So, you've seen the Cubs before?"

"Yes, my friend Yolanda's dad works for the Braves in Atlanta, so I get to go to quite a few games. I've seen the Cubs

They Say It's a River

Chapter Twenty-Eight

three times and got to watch Andre Dawson hit two balls out of the park. It should be a good game. I will say, I'm pretty happy they picked up Sammy Sosa from the White Sox this season."

"So am I. Have heard good things about him. I guess he was glad not to have to move cities again by switching to the Cubs."

As they slowed with traffic, exiting for the new Megamall in Gurnee, Leah watched the myriad of people streaming in.

"So, Jake, just so I can keep it straight, how is Bobby your Uncle?" She was still trying to figure out the family dynamics.

Jake thought for a second, "He's not exactly my Uncle. Christy is my cousin's-cousin, I think. Right, Grandpa?"

Alvin thought of the easiest way to clue Leah in. "Bobby's kind of married in, but we all love him. He's my brother's son-in-law. But it's easier to just have the kids call him Uncle Bobby at the gatherings, as there are a lot of Glasses and Stantons."

"What's he like?" asked Leah.

"Uncle Bobby, he's a lot of fun. Likes to tease, but not too much to upset Christy," said Jake

"Is she coming?" asked Leah.

"No, she's probably working at the salon today," Alvin ran his hand along the bare back of his head. "Not that I see her much, but she's a hairdresser. Bobby works in the Motorola plant. Something with semiconductor manufacturing, so he has a weird schedule, but he's off today."

"That's pretty cool, I never understood how they made them." Leah looked back at Jake.

"It is," Jake agreed but with a word of warning. "He really likes that stuff, if you want to talk about it, but make sure you really, really want to talk about it."

"Baseball is probably a safe topic," Alvin commented. "Jenny will be there. That sweet girl will probably talk your ear off and keep going."

"How old is she?" Leah inquired.

"She's twelve," Jake answered for her as he thought back to their conversation the other night.

"That's such a tough age," Leah agreed. "I remember

twelve. It sucked."

"I think it kind of does for everyone," said Alvin.

"You remember being twelve, Grandpa?"

"The time when I was twelve, I'll never forget," his voice reflected.

"Why's that?" Jake was confused, as he had not heard much of his grandfather's childhood.

"Maybe we don't have to talk about it." Leah realized there was more there that he may not want to talk about.

"It's okay, Leah," Alvin waxed into his nostalgia. "It was during the Great Depression. We lost the farm that year, like so many of our neighbors. That's when we moved in with family–into the house we live in to this day. We all worried that it would never end. Learned the appreciation of simply having food to eat." He went on telling of the struggles of those years and all the changes of the times.

The rest of the ride, Leah sat in an awkward silence, wondering about the things being shared that she knew from her own grandparents, but different in how things were in the North.

They took the Dempster exit and wound their way past the bungalows, row houses, and car dealerships until they reached Bobby's house.

As they pulled up, Bobby was standing outside in his usual blue-jean cap and a Cubs shirt, his day-old shave barely hidden. Jenny leaned against him, her shoulder-length, burnished-brown hair tumbled down her back in layers. She wore blue jeans and a pink t-shirt with a neon butterfly in flight on the front. She smiled and waved when she saw the Buick.

Leah's attention was drawn to Bobby, as he was turned back towards the house. From the garage emerged a man in his mid-forties. His light sandy brown hair was combed in a classic tapered style, revealing a slightly receding hairline on his square-shaped face. Amber aviator sunglasses hid his eyes, but a perfectly-trimmed golden goatee adorned his chin. His lips were pursed in a firm line that mirrored his posture, a stance so rigid you could plumb a wall with it.

Any calmness Leah had managed to cultivate evaporated.

Chapter Twenty-Eight

She replayed Bonnie's advice from the night before: "Jake's dad is all business."

"So, like an optimist, pessimist...?" She had asked

"Neither, He's a realist. In his own words."

"What the heck does that mean?"

"It means he doesn't let his feelings cloud his judgment. If something's good, he sees it. If it's bad, he sees it. He assesses the situation, follows his gut, and goes with it.'"

"So, first impressions are everything?"

"Leah, Leah, Leah. With that man, there is only one impression: his." The seriousness of Bonnie's face still burned in her mind.

"Great," Leah thought. "Just great."

She was jolted back to reality by Alvin breaking the silence. "Well, son, there's your dad. Best of luck, kid."

"Thanks, Grandpa," was all Jake could manage as they pulled to a stop. Paul Stanton turned and strode toward the car, his confidence as commanding as a judge entering a courtroom.

Chapter Twenty-Nine
Are You That Somebody?

Alvin opened the door and stepped out, arms outstretched for a hug with his son.

Paul pulled his father in. "Good to see you, Dad."

"You too, Paulie, good flight?"

"Not bad," Paul replied, glancing toward the young woman in the passenger seat, then his son getting out of the back. His voice became annoyed, "The kids didn't offer to drive?"

"Nah, I like the drive. Could do it in my sleep," Alvin said as Jake rounded the car.

"Hey, Dad," Jake said cautiously as he got closer.

His lack of confidence made Leah's stomach churn, leaving her wondering what she'd gotten herself into.

"Jacob." A soft smile crinkled his eyes as he embraced his son. "Good to see you. You've been doing okay at the cottage?"

"Yeah, Dad."

"Bobby said it looked pretty sharp when they were up there last weekend," Paul commented.

"I've had a bunch of help," Jake answered. "Spent most of yesterday painting because it's supposed to rain tomorrow."

With that, Leah figured it was now or never and opened her door, stepping out into the overcast Chicago day.

Not waiting for introductions, Paul turned toward her and made his own. "You must be Betty's niece. Call me 'Paul', as there's only one 'Mr. Stanton', in my opinion," he grinned at Alvin. "And you are?"

Leah was caught off guard and momentarily forgot her own name, "I'm Leah, Mr...umm, Paul, it's nice to meet you. Thank you for the tickets today. I love watching baseball."

"I like this one, Jake," Paul tossed the words at his

Chapter Twenty-Nine

son, "She actually *likes* baseball." This earned a chuckle from everyone. Leah could only guess who he was referring to. "I'm glad you're joining us today. I hope my son has been the gentleman he knows to be."

"Yes, he and Bonnie and I have had a bit of fun on the lake when we're not working at the diner," Leah replied.

"Oh my gosh," Paul chuckled. "Clara's still roping any relative half-close to standing still into working at that diner. Some night after she's had a beer or two, you should ask your aunt about working there back in the sixties."

"Oh, I'll remember that," Leah glanced at Jake, unsure what to make of Paul's comment.

"Okay, people, let's get rolling. Traffic's only gonna get worse," Bobby waved everyone to the van. "You said your friend gave you a parking pass?"

Paul reached into his pocket and pulled out a form. "Gave me directions to pull into a side-alley off Cornelia and give them this piece of paper he faxed me."

"Alright, load up. Jenny in the way back, please," Bobby directed his daughter as he got into the driver's seat.

"I can get in the way back," Leah offered. "I don't mind."

"You sure?" Jake asked.

"I'm good," Leah confirmed, climbing into the back seat. "Hi, Jenny, I'm Leah."

"Hi," Jenny took in the older girl with the long raven-black locks. "Your hair is *sooo* pretty! My mom would love it."

"Thank you," Leah moved her hand through her hair, settling it more on her right shoulder. "Your shirt is cute. Do you like butterflies?"

"Yes! This is one of my favorites," Jenny opened her jean jacket so Leah could see it better. "I love that it's hot pink and has hot pink in the butterflies. I have several butterfly shirts and even some cool butterfly patches I put on my jean jacket."

"That's awesome," Leah admired the patches stretching out on the elbow. "Do you like baseball?"

"A little bit," Jenny admitted. "My dad loves the Cubs. Do you?"

Are You That Somebody?

"Yes, I try to see games as often as I can. I enjoy going to the ballpark. Each one has its own uniqueness. Wrigley is one of the oldest in baseball, so I'm pretty excited."

"I'm glad you're here today. Now I have another girl to talk to. Normally it's just boys."

"Well, I'm glad I'm here too."

In the front seat, Bobby looked back to Paul, "Paulie, where are these seats at?"

"Section eighteen. Box seats, right behind home plate."

"Your friend isn't using them?" Bobby questioned.

"Don't know about *'friend'*. Donaldson just got a sweetheart deal from us that keeps the wheel turning, which my wife is going to murder me over, so getting tickets as part of the deal sweetens the margin of loss we're taking."

"How is Cindy doing?" Alvin wondered, as he often did about a relationship he and Lucy never understood .

"She's made a lot of progress, some things are just going to take time," Paul replied, choosing to keep the messaging positive about his wife. "She gets her two-year coin next month."

"That's great, I'm glad you all are doing better."

"It's still a struggle, but we're getting there..." His voice trailed off. "Thanks for asking, Dad. I know you and Cindy haven't always seen eye-to-eye, but we've been through a lot over the years and we're getting through this, too."

A few minutes of quiet passed before Jake decided to add to the prior comment. "We had a good talk the other night."

"I heard," Paul nodded as he recalled the conversation from a day earlier. "And I appreciate that. And I'm glad you're here for the summer, helping your grandfather and..." he lowered his voice to his son, "making friends."

"Dad..." Jake blushed a little surprised that was said with Leah right behind them.

As they pulled into the side alley, a guy who looked better-suited to be a bouncer for a biker bar walked up, "You're in the wrong alley."

Bobby handed him the piece of paper and the guy studied it before handing it back. "Okay, if Mr. Donaldson's good, I'm

Chapter Twenty-Nine

good. Drive past the building, there's a side lot, and Tats will get you parked."

"Thanks, friend." Bobby drove forward and past the building.

"Tats," Jake started to ask, "How are we gonna know the right..." He stopped short as "Tats" came into view. He wore a bright array of tattoos decorating his large arms, visible chest, and bald head.

He looked at Bobby, "Pass?"

Bobby gave him the paper, which he scrutinized for a minute, "Tell Mr. Donaldson, 'Hello'. Alright, everybody out! I'll get this bad-boy parked."

They all got out, watching Tats wheel and park the car among the other vehicles with expertise that would impress any stunt driver. After completing his parking magic, he handed the keys back to Bobby, "Enjoy the game!"

When they were a ways away, Jenny pulled her dad's hand, "So, is our car safe?"

"Those men all work for Donaldson and are aware I know him personally," Paul chuckled. "I'd feel sorry for anyone who would think of causing trouble with those two."

They soon had programs, a foam finger for Jenny, popcorn, and a couple of smokies. The concourse was alive with the smells and sounds that seemed to speak of a different era. Spotting two drink hawkers by the box seats entrance, Alvin and Bobby got beers. Jake got a Dr. Pepper and Jenny, Paul, and Leah opted for Diet Pepsi.

On the steps down, they discovered the seats were split across two rows. Leah looked at Jake and suggested they could switch up later in the game.

Bobby took a seat with Jenny sitting between him and Leah. Alvin and Paul sat together with Jake on the end.

Jake and Paul took a look at the lineup. "No frills today." Paul remarked as he filled in his scorecard in the program. With Vizcaino leading off, then Dascenzo, and Sandberg, the Cubs were sticking with what had been working as of late.

"So, how was the trip?" Jake asked as Paul handed him

some popcorn."

"Not too bad. The Donaldsons drive a hard bargain, but we need them for shipping. He's putting a lot more into Chicago and moving most of their offices out of Detroit. The usual, just trying to keep margins to cover costs and make a little profit so your grandfather and mother don't lose their minds. My bigger question is, what's going on with you, son?"

"I mean, you told your mom you were going to do the interview but told her your heart was in the Midwest," his eyes traveled to the girl sitting below them.

"Does the reason for your heart shifting to the Midwest have anything to do with current trends? Or are you just trying to get away?"

"Dad, when you turned eighteen, you packed your bags and went across the country," Jake said. "And you went to school and met Mom, and then you helped Grandpa build the business. Now you're successful and making big money. I just want that same chance. I—"

"Whoa, there," Paul slowed him. "There's a lot of leaps between all that, you know? We lived pretty meagerly those first few years, broke as church mice. And when you came along, I was sure we were going under. We stabilized a little and, a few years later, your brother came along. We barely made it.

"And, yes, thankfully, things started to pick up, but the hours were killer. I feel like your grandmother raised you more than we did," Paul said, shaking his head. "All that rough scramble of being so broke we had to count out each item we tossed in the cart to make sure we could pay for what we needed to survive.

"Thankfully, we succeeded enough to reap the rewards, but those early years are something I rather you not have to endure," Paul finished.

"I know, Dad, but I want to do something with events and live music," Jake saw his father raise his eyebrows and quickly continued.

"Not trying to be a musician but, like, being part of that whole scene of event management. And some of mom's cousins

Chapter Twenty-Nine

live in Toledo and it's not too far away from Wisconsin and I just want to be me."

"Now, where have I heard those words before?" Alvin elbowed his son.

"Dad," Paul muttered, hoping he would stay out of this one.

"Just saying this sounds familiar," Alvin reflected before going back to watching the ballgame.

"And what else?" Paul asked.

"I'm worried about Stanford. I mean, I do okay, Dad, but I'm not smart like Susan and Laura. Susan could go to Stanford on a full-ride, per what Curtis has been saying, and she'll blow them all away. I'm worried I'd go, crash and burn, and fail out."

"I think Ohio State or Indiana might be more my speed and they have solid programs in business," Jake said. "I want to go work hard, Dad, get a job at the events center wherever I go and learn how it works. Like you and Mom did with the mining industry, traveling all over the planet to see what you could find and discovering new avenues and making money on new projects and going after new mineral ideas. That paid off, but you did it yourself."

Paul listened to his son with a little pride. "I'm glad to hear that, son. It sounds like you've actually thought this out. Now, I have to ask. Did you really tell your mother the only thing you figured out on the expensive calculator she bought you was how to play that Hitchhiker's Guide to the Galaxy game that Susan loaded for you?"

"Yes. I was just being honest and she actually laughed," And said she wasn't surprised. I mean, of the many classes I take, my grades in math are not great."

"From my observation, your primary study for most of this year was Marta," Paul dryly assessed. "And I think you failed that exam."

"Ouch. Jeez, thanks, Dad," Jake feigned a wound to his ego from the stinging comment.

"You're welcome," Paul patted his shoulder. "We'll talk more about this in a bit. It's been a pretty slow game so far,

Are You That Somebody?

mostly a pitcher's battle. Hope the girls aren't too bored."

Chapter Thirty
Centerfield

A row below, Jenny and Leah were in full conversation.

"So, what's Georgia like?"

"It's kind of like here, just a lot warmer and with more hills. As you get up into Tennessee, there are the mountains. That's where I like to go. Actually, I have a picture." Leah got out her purse and flipped open a little red leather photo album to a worn picture of the Ocoee Valley.

"Wow, that's really gorgeous"

"It is. You can see all the way to Georgia from there and some of North Carolina on a clear day."

"Cool. Oh, is that your mom? She is really pretty; you sure look like her," said Jenny.

"Thank you." Leah was caught off guard and unsure how much she wanted to say, or how emotional she should get at the ballpark. "That is a picture of my mom. I was about your age when we took that picture. We were up in the Great Smoky Mountains that summer. My dad wanted us to go and hike some of the Appalachian Trail and see Looking Glass Falls."

"Did you go to Dollywood?"

"No, we skipped Pigeon Forge," Leah answered. "My mom didn't like super touristy stuff."

"The outdoors are my favorite, too. One of the cousins has a bunch of land in the U.P. It's so green, the hills go on forever, and there is a lake that is clear like glass, you can see all the way to the bottom."

"That is wild."

A foul ball that went straight into the net in front of them grabbed their attention and Jenny remembered a question her mom had asked her earlier. "There is something I can't figure

Centerfield

out, cause I know a lot of people at the lake. How are you related to Bonnie and Ms. Clara?"

"You know Aunt Clara?"

"Everyone who goes to Bass Lake knows Ms. Clara and she knows everybody," said Jenny with awe.

"That she does," Leah shook her head. "Well, my mom's second cousin is Bonnie's dad."

"Oh, okay. Are you up here for the whole summer?"

"No, just 'til the end of June."

"I bet your mom misses you."

The comment struck Leah and she tried to hold it, sucking in a breath to keep a tear from slipping out..

"I'm sorry. I didn't mean to make you cry," Jenny apologized.

"It's okay. Want to go with me to the washroom? I'll get us a snack and we can talk," Leah commented as she got up from her seat. Jenny quickly got up behind her. She told her dad, "Leah and I are gonna go up to the bathroom. We'll be back."

"Okay, thanks for going with her, Leah," said Bobby.

"You're welcome," said Leah as they went up the steps.

As they passed, Jake looked at Bobby. "Where are they going?"

"The washroom. I didn't give them twenty-questions. I'm sure they'll be back," said Bobby shaking his head.

Walking up the first-base side, Leah composed herself. They found a quiet spot by a pretzel stand. They split the pretzel and Leah looked at Jenny, "My mom died six months ago."

"I'm so sorry, no one told me," said Jenny.

"I try not to talk about it too much. I mean, I'm sure Alvin knows because Clara and Lucy talk far more than they should, in my opinion. But it still hits sometimes in unexpected ways. Yes, she was beautiful, with her long auburn hair. She had a laugh that still rings in my ear. I miss her and it still hurts."

"I bet it does. I can't imagine my mom being gone. I don't know what I would do. Or my dad. He would lose it," Jenny reflected quietly.

"My dad kind of fell apart, which is why I'm here. I have

Chapter Thirty

to move to Texas after I get back and I really don't want to go. Now everything has changed, and I can't change it back. All I can say is love your mom with all your heart," She put her hand on Jenny's shoulder. "Give her a big hug later. Time is precious and you never know how long you've got. So you have to cherish the moments that you have, you know?"

"I do," Jenny whispered as she clutched her elbows, rocking a little.

"I appreciate you letting me talk with you about it."

"I'm glad you told me. I hope you have a good trip while you're here."

"Thank you, I will. And I was wondering, do you think your family likes me?" Leah was curious about what Jenny had heard.

"Don't you worry, I'll make sure they do," Jenny gave her a grin. "I'll talk to my mom."

"Thank you, Jenny. Your mom is close with everyone?"

"My mom is a hairdresser. She takes care of everyone in the family, including Grandma Lucy, who she sees this Thursday," Jenny winked.

"You know, I think we are gonna be good friends," Leah said as they walked back down the concourse to rejoin the boys.

"So, Dad, do you mind if I sit with my friend?" Jake looked at the two open seats in front of them.

"I guess, son. And, before I forget, here is Mr. Carroll's card," he handed Jake the lawyer's number. Paul moved down to sit opposite Bobby, leaving an open seat at the end for both Jenny and Leah.

Leah couldn't help but laugh as they walked down the steps. "Look, Jenny, I think Jake wants me to sit by him." She pointed to the change in the seating arrangements.

Jenny sat down and gave her dad a hug. "I love you, Daddy. I'm glad I'm here with you today," her eyes shining bright.

"And I love you, too, sweetheart," he hugged her. "I'm glad you came today. We don't get to do this often." His heart warmed at the thought of the nice day with just him and his

Centerfield

daughter and how rare those would probably be in the future.

Leah looked at Jake and Alvin with a smirk as she sat down in the open seat. "So, I guess I'm sitting by you, *Farmer Tan*," her voice rubbed with southern sassiness.

"If the lady would choose to," Jake drawled, playing along.

"The lady does," Leah leaned into Jake along with her tone. Below, Paul laughed out loud.

"That one's gonna be dangerous," he whispered to Bobby.

"From what Evelyn told Christy, he follows those two girls around like a puppy," Bobby confirmed.

"And that would be my son," Paul reflected. "God help me if he can't stay out of trouble for a month."

"Well, we shall see. I'll keep you posted." Bobby turned back to the game.

Things livened up in the top of the fourth as Lankford cracked one out of the park. The score was one to zero, St. Louis.

The crowd was awake now and, as the Cubs went back up to bat, the crowd began to cheer. "Enjoying the ballgame?" Leah asked Jake.

"Oh yeah, hopefully Sandberg will get farther than second base," Jake motioned to the field. They watched another out before Andre Dawson strutted up to the plate and put one in deep right field. Sandberg rounded third and just made it home, bringing the game to a tie.

"Now we're talking about a ball game," Leah clapped.

Jake's heart fluttered a little. "I love that you love baseball."

"What's not to love?" Leah gave a teasing look. The fifth inning became another pitchers' battle. Jake was ready to stretch his legs and asked Leah if she wanted to walk around and see the stadium.

"The history here is amazing," Leah looked around at the plaques as they walked along the concourse on the third baseline toward the gift shop. Leah made a beeline to an oversized t-shirt with an expansive caricature of Harry Caray saying, "Holy

Chapter Thirty

Cow". Jake tried on a few Cub's hats as they perused the varying memorabilia.

Jake heard his stomach growl as he looked through the collector mugs, "Wanna go sit down and get something to eat?"

"Sure," Leah agreed as they paid the cashier. Jake passed on the hat, but the Harry Caray shirt was going back to Atlanta.

They took in all the vendor options and found their way down the first base concourse to a hamburger stand.

"What do you want? My treat."

"You sure?"

"Of course. What will you have?"

"Hamburger with everything but onions," Jake decided.

"You got it, boss," the grill master tossed a fresh patty on the grill. "And you, missy?"

"I'll have a smoked dog, full Chicago-style," Leah told him after seeing the previous customer's order.

"Coming right up," was his answer as they got their fountain drinks.

They found an open table on the deep right-field patio, looking out across the stadium. The camera was panning around the stands as the Cubs took the field at the top of the sixth inning.

"So, thank you again, Jake, for inviting me. I really appreciate it."

"You are welcome. I'm glad you came," Jake struggled to find the right words. "Bonnie isn't big into baseball and, I don't know, I was curious if you would go."

"Curious if I would go?" Leah quizzically scanned his face.

"I mean, I didn't know what you would say," said Jake.

"Really?" Leah was taken aback. "To be honest, Farmer Tan, I was surprised you asked me. I thought you'd ask Bonnie, as you've known each other for years."

"But, I, umm, thought it would be fun to take you 'cause you've never been, and..."

Leah enjoyed watching the boy struggle around his answer. "And..."

"And I wanted to go with you," Jake gave an unsure

glance.

"Really?" Leah faked surprise and leaned toward him across the table. "Why?"

"Well, you're not gonna like both reasons," Jake spoke without thinking.

"Hmmm, maybe you should stop while you're ahead there," Lean wondered what the boy was going to say.

"I figured if I took you, my dad would be on better behavior with a total stranger than he would be with Bonnie here."

"Wow, those are some really heartfelt words there," Leah flushed, getting a little fiery that she was brought as a prop to stave off Jake getting ripped by his dad. She got up from her seat and turned toward the concourse.

"But wait," Jake tried to pull the conversation out of its current tailspin."There is one reason I really wanted you to come,"

"And what, pray tell, would that be?" Leah spun towards him, still a little offended.

"I've enjoyed getting to know you the past few days and I wanted the chance to get to know you more," Jake tried to entreat her to come sit down.

"And why is that?" She put her hands on hips, annoyed at the cliched line.

"Because when I'm with you, you make me feel like it's okay to just be me," Jake quietly added.

As the crowd around them faded, all Leah heard was his voice.

She shook herself out of it to deliver a snappy comeback. "I bet you say that to all the girls."

Jake looked into her eyes as he extended his hand, "No, I can't explain it but, with you, it's different."

She took his hand and he pulled her close, both lost within the depths of each other.

Across the field, Jenny shouted, "Look, it's Jake!"

"Where?" Paul looked up to see that there, on the Jumbotron was his son and the Georgia girl, eye to eye, with a

Chapter Thirty-One

look that Paul had seen a time or two.

"I guess there's your answer on the girl," Bobby elbowed Paul.

Paul just shook his head. "Wonderful," he groaned, wadding up his empty popcorn.

Chapter Thirty-One
Who's Gonna Ride Your Wild Horses

The cheering of the crowd and the 'Awwww' sounds around them brought Leah back to reality.

"Oh, crap!" She saw they were on the Jumbotron. With an awkward motion, they waved until the camera went off them.

"I wonder if my dad saw that," Jake glanced around like he was just waking up to reality.

"The whole freaking stadium just saw it. And you are blushing." Leah poked his chest.

"So are you, a little," Jake's eyes danced at hers.

"I've just gotten a little sun," Leah looked to make sure the camera was off of them for good.

At the bottom of the sixth inning, they made their way back around the concourse to their seats, stopping to watch Sandberg crack one out of the park as the crowd went wild.

"I am so embarrassed," Leah groaned as they watched the home run replay on the Jumbotron.

"Why?" Jake asked, trying to downplay it all a little.

"Let's see, the whole world just watched me and you doing whatever that was." Leah began walking ahead of him.

"And what was that?" Jake called out to her.

"I don't know, having a moment." She threw her arms in the air. "A loss of presence-of-mind, obviously."

"Obviously," Jake repeated sarcastically, not sure where this was going.

"Would you slow down, please?" he hurried to catch up.

"Why?" Leah walked faster.

Chapter Thirty-One

"Because," Jake said as he got close to walking even with her. "If you get back before me, they'll really talk. The game is almost over."

"Okay," Leah slowed down.

"So, what is our story?" Jake asked when they reached the steps to take them down to their seats.

"We can say I was sharing with you about all that's going on and we got caught up in the moment. Jenny will understand and she'll cover for us," Leah told him.

"Oh, sure. I follow you," Jake nodded, being completely unsure and not following at all, but deciding to just go with it.

"Okay, here goes," she waited until there was a distraction on the field and they slipped back down to their seats.

"Well, hello, you two, glad you could join us," Paul flashed a wicked grin at his son.

"Leah wanted to look around. There's a lot to discover here," Jake motioned to the expansive stadium.

"Oh, I'm sure," Paul replied, just loud enough for Jake to hear him.

Jenny turned to Leah, "We saw you on the Jumbotron, that was so cute."

"Jake and I were sharing a moment about something," Leah gave a look to Jenny, who followed her inference, 'Ohh,' and then she looked up at Jake.

"That is sweet of you, Jake."

"What's sweet?" Bobby asked his daughter.

"I'll tell you later, Dad,"

"Oh, okay," Bobby went back to the game.

The pitchers' battle soon ended, and the Cubs were able to hold the slim lead of 2-1 through the top of the ninth. Paul mentioned starting to head back as the crowd began to thin.

When they got to the lot, they watched as Tats expertly maneuvered the van out for them and, soon, they finished the slow drive back to Skokie. Jenny and Leah went inside the house before they hit the road, as Christy wanted to meet Leah before they left.

As Bobby reloaded the van, Paul walked over to his son,

Who's Gonna Ride Your Wild Horses

"Jake, walk with me a minute."

"Sure, Dad." They began a short walk up the gray stamped concrete.

"I'm glad we were able to do this today. We don't get to do this much anymore and we should really try to more often. And I really appreciate you taking the initiative to call the lawyer and set that up. I know you have other ideas, but I don't want you blowing off your senior year," Paul expressed his urgency to his son. "I want to see you really put in a bit more effort into your grades. I look forward to being out here in a few weeks."

Paul's expression became serious for a moment. He stopped, looking Jake in the eye. "I'm glad you're getting a chance to make your own memories, especially with Aunt Edith. That means so much to me and to your grandfather. And, as for your friend, she seems like a nice girl but be wise, okay, son?"

"Okay, Dad, I will. Thanks for today," Jake pulled his father into a hug. "Have a safe flight. I love you."

"Thank you, son. I love you too," Paul glanced at this watch. "You're driving right? Your grandfather is pretty tired."

"I planned to."

"Thank you, son."

Leah was back outside, walking toward the Buick. "It was nice to meet you…Paul."

"And it was nice to meet you, too, Leah," Paul reached out, shaking her hand. "I hope you enjoy the rest of your trip."

"I will."

"Bobby, are you ready to hit O'Hare traffic one more time today?"

"Sure, what else am I gonna do?" he laughed as they got into the van and drove away.

They all waved as Christy came outside and gave Jake another of her enveloping hugs.

"Have a safe trip back, Jacob."

"Thank you, Aunt Christy."

"And you, dear. May God bless you and hold your heart, child."

She reached for the girl and tucked into an embrace as

Chapter Thirty-One

if she was her own, holding her close as Leah whispered back, "Thank you."

"Well, Grandpa, are you ready to go? I'll drive home so you can take a nap in the back seat if you want," Jake asked, seeing his grandfather yawning.

"Thank you, sounds fantastic," Alvin stretched as he handed Jake the keys.

After the last goodbyes, Jake and Leah got in the front. Alvin took the pillow provided by Christy and made himself comfortable against the side in the back seat.

As they crossed the state line, Jake looked at Leah and asked, "What are you smiling about?"

"You have a beautiful family. It makes me smile. You dad wasn't as terrifying as he was made out to be."

"That reference would be a stronger picture of my mother," Jake admitted. "I'm glad he was on good behavior today."

"Only 'cause you brought me as a buffer. Still not sure how to feel about that," her voice was dry.

"Shhh," Jake moved his finger to his lips.

"If you're worried about your grandfather, he's sound asleep. And has been since Waukegan. I do have to say that Jenny is a sweet girl."

"She sure connected with you."

"I kind of opened up with her a little more than I planned. You know, about my mom."

"I'm sorry about that," Jake interjected. " Bonnie had told—"

"Don't be sorry," Leah retorted, then slowed her reply. "It's not gonna change that she's gone."

"I know, I'm just not sure what to say."

"No one is," Leah let out a breath. "No one ever is. And, Jake, it's okay. You don't have to know what to say."

The car was quiet between them, aside from Alvin's snoring, until they crossed the Root River.

"You told me that you feel you can be yourself with me. Well, I'll try to be more of myself around you," Leah moved her hand to his shoulder.

"Wait, you're not really just flirty and sarcastic?" Jake gave her a toothy grin.

Leah simmered for a moment. "You know, Farmer Tan..."

"What, Leah?"

Leah snapped her hand back to her lap. "Someday you're gonna learn to shut your mouth while you're ahead."

A deep laugh erupted from the back seat. Jake and Leah exchanged glances as the Milwaukee skyline came into view.

Chapter Thirty-Two
Keep on Walkin'

Traffic was light on Swan Boulevard after Jake dropped Alvin off and made his way back to the interstate. Sitting at the red light, the smell of a nearby BBQ drifted into his nose and mind.

"Hey, Leah, you hungry?"

"A little." Leah was slouched in the front seat, her eyes glazed over from the ride and all the sun from the ballgame. "What are you thinking?"

"Have you had any deep-dish yet?"

"No, I've heard about it, but never tried it."

Jake got an unsettling look in his eye and made a U-turn, in the style of *21 Jump Street*, pointing the car toward Bluemound.

"What the heck, man?" Leah, now alert and hanging onto the grab handle, tried to ease back into her seat. "Where are we going?"

"Chicago pizza you want, Chicago pizza I deliver," Jake tried his best maître d' impression.

"Just don't kill me in the process, okay?"

"Your safety is my top priority." He gave her an indignant glance.

"Just keep your eyes on the road, Jeeves."

Pulling into the parking lot, the bright red and green sign of Rocky Rococo's greeted them. Leah could smell the baked dough and garlic roasting and her stomach agreed it was hungry, too.

An Original Chicago was soon in the oven. They sipped their drinks in a corner booth, Leah taking in the homestyle nature of the establishment.

Keep On Walkin'

"I can see why you like this place. It's simple."

"Simply good pizza." Jake flipped the table card to see what other specials sounded good. "The boys love this place. Brian and Matt would eat here five days a week if they could."

"Today was fun." Leah looked at Jake as he sat across the table. "Even if I am just a human shield to you."

"Hey, I told you it was more than that."

"Only after I got up to leave." Leah eyed him, looking for any answers in his face that his words weren't sharing. "Makes a girl wonder about the sincerity of it."

The pizza soon arrived and Jake offered to cut it in the pan and serve her.

"As for being flirty and sarcastic, I can play that hand with my eyes closed and you wouldn't know what games we were playing." Leah dug her knife into the thick crust, twirling her fork to make a long strand of cheese cooperate.

As she savored the explosion of flavors in her mouth, her eyes settled back on the boy across the table, his eyes unmoved from hers.

Leah pointed her fork at him. "But here's the thing: I'm tired of all that. I've played that game for the last year-plus and I don't have it in me right now. So, then the question for you is, what's your game?"

Jake pushed his fork into another slice as he tried to think of an answer. In his mind, this was part of the fun–the game. He'd trudged through the whole to-do list and expectations of his relationship with Marta for the last year and a half. The fun, the flirting, and playful sarcasm that burned early-on had long-since died. And now he was free for something new. Looking back into the icy blues that he longed to melt, he tossed a little fire.

"I think the game can be half the fun."

"Provided both know the game they're playing." Leah's eyes met his, a glow behind them that seemed to hint that a fire had been lit.

"What are you up for?" Jake slyly answered with a teasing glance at her as he tossed the softball question, only to

Chapter Thirty-Two

watch it get scorched before reaching the plate.

"So that's all it is?" she spat. "Thanks for clarifying." She got up and went to the bathroom to calm her spirit for a minute.

Jake sat at the table, wondering how this had gotten so far off track and how he could get it back on.

Five minutes passed before Leah returned and finished her pizza, the squeak of her silverware on the glass plate speaking for her.

Jake got out cash for the tip, but she waved him off, "I've got it," being her only words.

The pizza was boxed up into two, as Jake knew if Leah passed on it, Bonnie would eat some. If Joe didn't make it a snack before morning, that is.

The quiet drive screamed in Jake's brain as he ran line after line in his head, but none left his lips. Leah looked out the window, seeming to follow her own inner monologue.

As they got near Bonnie's house in Waukesha, Jake decided to take a drive by the Riverwalk. Pulling into a parking spot, Leah was awoken from her mental conversation.

"You are a few blocks early to be stopping."

"I just wanted to walk with you for a minute. It's pretty along the river this time of day."

"I'm sure it is, Farmer Tan. But I don't feel much like talking." She cast a glance and saw hope in his eyes that she would reconsider. She exited the car and caught his eye with a look of frustration. "Fine. How about this? I'll give you until that curve to make whatever case you're going for." Leah pointed to where the footpath turned toward the bridge that crossed the Fox River.

"Okay. Sounds Good." Jake followed her as they began walking.

"So?" she quizzed.

"I understand that you're tired of games; trust me, I am too. I know your world is turned upside down, and it sucks and hurts, but—" Jake drew a breath.

"There's always a 'but.'" Leah stopped and stared into

Keep on Walkin'

his eyes. "What's yours?"

"You don't have to lose your love for life, even though you've lost someone within it." Jake reached toward her, but his words and hand fell short.

"You know nothing." Leah pulled her hand away. "You know nothing at all." She turned, walking briskly toward the bridge.

"Leah, we're like five blocks from their house."

Leah slowed down enough so he could hear her clearly. "Then I guess I'll keep on walkin'."

Jake watched till she faded from view as she turned onto Bonnie's street.

Upstairs, at the Stanton house, Jake paced the worn floral rug as the line rang four times before Bonnie answered.

"Hello," came a half-cognizant voice over the line.

"Hey, Bonnie, I wanted to call, and—"

Bonnie cut him short. "Explain to me why you made my cousin walk home. What the heck, Jake? I'm turning on my street after working twelve hours at the diner and there is my cousin bawling her eyes out, shuffling down the sidewalk. I get her in the car and she tells me everything that you said. Everything. I get you're a guy and emotionally tone-deaf, but wow, this time you even surprised me. Did you really tell her to just get over her mom and move on? Do you have any fricken clue what is going on in her life right now? Are you taking notes, cause you should be.

"I know you have all these wild dreams floating in that neanderthal brain of yours, but you need to take a minute from life on planet Jake and realize where that actually fits into the rest of the universe."

Jake had rehearsed his planned speech for Bonnie so she would get Leah on the phone, but the nouns and verbs were scrambled in his brain by her verbal assault.

"I didn't make her walk," he finally pieced together.

"You didn't give her much choice. You pulled your classic, gonna take a nice walk and talk some sense move."

"I think she misunderstood what I was trying to say."

Chapter Thirty-Two

"You think," Bonnie clipped.

"Could you see if she's still up? I would like to try talking with her, explain, you know."

"No," came the cold reply.

"Come on, Bonnie, I could use your help here."

A laugh of disbelief met his words. "My help? You want my help? I put my own feelings aside and laid out a clear path, talking about how great you are. Then the stars align and you are gifted box-seat Cubs tickets for a girl who would rather read the Baseball Digest over Seventeen. And in a miracle-of-miracles, you blow it. It's mystifying."

"I wasn't trying to upset her."

"Maybe you need to think more clearly on what you are actually trying to do. But, it's late, I'm tired, and going to bed. Give me a call in the morning, I'll see what way the wind is blowing, okay."

"Okay, thanks, Bonnie."

"Don't thank me yet. And Jake."

"Yeah?"

"Don't tell people what they should be looking for when you don't have a clue what they've lost."

" I know." Jake sat on the edge of the couch, worrying out his emotions on the old fabric with his free hand.

"I know you do," Bonnie's voice softened. "Get some rest too, okay. Night."

"Night."

Chapter Thirty-Three
Into the Fire

Jake picked up the phone, dialed, and waited.

"Hello," came Bonnie's groggy voice.

"Good morning,"

"Do you know what time it is?"

"It's nine a.m."

"Exactly," Bonnie shook the cobwebs out of her brain, "I was still sleeping."

"Still? I've been up since.."

"Oh, I'm sure you've been up since 5:30 with your grandmother," interrupted Bonnie. "Reminder, I worked for twelve hours yesterday at the diner. Most of it, running the grill by myself , and then spending my evening consoling my cousin about you being a clueless jerk."

"Woah, there,"Jake stopped her. "Is that what she said?"

"No, you are so dense. That's a condensed version, she said a lot more."

"Fabulous," thought Jake.

"But now that I'm awake, what do you want?"

"Natalie and I are talking about a movie today and we were wondering if you would want to go."

"Who's going?"

"It will probably be all the kids, so the movie selections in discussion are FernGully, Sister Act, or Beauty and the Beast."

"I'd see Beauty and the Beast again, and Sister Act looks amazing. I've heard it's got some violence in it, though. How old is Nicky?"

"Just turned six. I know Natalie had talked about Sister Act, as well. The boys might like it, too. So, I'm not sure about Nick. Maybe we'll do FernGully. I'll find out."

Chapter Thirty-Three

"What time are you going?"

"Probably around 1:30 to 2."

"When the princess awakens, I'll ask her if she's up to seeing you today."

"Thanks Bonnie, I'd like to finish the other half of that conversation."

"Let's see if you get a conversation first, goodnight," the click of the phone and a dial tone, let Jake know the call was over.

Jake looked around the room, and began to sort through what to wear for the day.

Around eleven, the Stanton house was bustling, Lucy talking with Natalie as the three boys ran around the backyard.

"Okay, so what time do you think you'll be back?" Lucy asked her eldest grandchildren.

"If we get to the pizza place by noon, we should be able to see a movie at two. So, around five, Grandma," Jake answered after thinking through the movies times they had looked at in the paper earlier

"How much do you think you'll need?" Lucy reached for her brown leather purse that hung from the banister.

"Five matinées and two buckets of popcorn and soda will probably be like thirty, and lunch, maybe twenty five," Jake counted out behind them.

"Here's sixty. If it's more, can you cover it?"

"Sure, Grandma," Jake assured her.

"Thank you. Just let me know later. I'll be out with the women's Rotary for the afternoon."

Jake slipped the cash into his HammerTime wallet. "Hey Nat, I'll be right back."

Jake slipped upstairs and hit redial on the cordless.

"Hello," came a southern voice on the other end of the line.

"Hey, Leah."

"What are you calling for, Farmer Tan?" her voice stewed in the emotions of the prior day.

"Did you and Bonnie want to go with us to the movies?"

"One question."
"Sure."
"What game are you playing?"
"None."
"And why is that?"
"Because, you deserve better." Jake let his words land as he stared into the phone hoping to hear an answer and not a dial tone.

"Good answer." He heard her breath muffle over the phone. "A movie might be fun. What time?"

"We should be at Mayfair around one-thirty-ish, after we do lunch."

"Okay, hang on. Let me ask her." He heard footsteps in the background. "He's catching a two o'clock," she yelled down the hall. "What? Okay. I'll tell him." Leah made her way back to the phone on the bed. "We'll meet you at the theater. Sound good?"

"Sounds good. See you there." Jake put down the phone and looked up to see Natalie standing at the top of the landing.

"Hey Nat."

"So, inviting company to the movie?" Natalie cocked an eyebrow.

"I thought it would be nice to invite them. I thought you liked Bonnie?" Jake appealed, knowing her being against this would be a wrench in any plans for the afternoon. .

"I do. Didn't you just spend the whole day with Leah yesterday?"

"Yes, and I'd like them to join us today."

"You aren't going to ditch us and leave me with the boys in the movie, right?" Natalie watched his eyes for an answer. "What are we gonna see anyway?"

"What about FernGully?"

"Dad doesn't like it. It's political. He doesn't disagree with it, in concept, but doesn't like that it's pushed in a kids' movie," Natalie explained, giving a condensed version of her father's lecture.

"I get that," Jake knew his uncle and his societal lectures

Chapter Thirty-Three

well. "What about Sister Act?"

"I do want to see that, but that's probably too much for Nicky. Isn't she hiding from the mafia or something?"

"We can figure it out there."

"Okay, ready to go?"

"Yup," Jake answered as they headed downstairs.

"Alright, boys, let's go," She called into the back yard, as they loaded up and headed for the pizza shop.

At twenty-after-one, Jake, Natalie, and the boys made their way into the theater and, there, standing in a pose by the cutout poster of Michelle Pfeiffer as Catwoman, was Leah.

"Good afternoon, Natalie. You get the boys enough pizza?" Leah walked over to the group.

"Two large pizzas and I barely got a piece," Natalie lamented. "Is Bonnie not here?"

"Bonnie's getting snacks. I was keeping an eye out for you all. What are you seeing?"

"There is still a bit of a debate. Matt, Brian, and I want to see Sister Act, but Nicky probably shouldn't." Natalie and Leah looked over at the six-year-old, who had wandered to the cutout of a giant toddler towering over Rick Moranis.

Leah thought for a second before seeing Jake angling to get her attention with a pointed finger to her and thumbs up. There were worse ways to spend an afternoon, she thought, and mouthed, "I guess" to Jake.

"Natalie, what if Jake and I take Nicky to see a movie, like Beauty and the Beast?" Leah asked her. "Bonnie can choose which she wants to see."

Natalie gave her cousin a suspicious look, then turned to Nick. "Nicky, would you be okay with that?"

"Sure," Nick agreed, taking Jake's hand.

"Okay," Natalie replied, not thrilled she was about to get stuck watching the boys for the afternoon. "I'm curious what Bonnie thinks."

"What I think about what?" Bonnie returned, balancing slurpees and a popcorn, which she handed to Leah.

"Jake has valiantly volunteered to go see Beauty and the

Into the Fire

Beast with Nick and Leah has offered to go with him," Natalie updated her with a touch of sarcasm. "So I can take the older boys to see Sister Act."

"You want to join us?" Leah asked her cousin, now getting mixed thoughts on seeing the movie with Jake..

"As much fun as being a third wheel sounds," Bonnie teased, "I'll go see Sister Act with you, Natalie. Have fun, cuz."

Nick tugged at Jake's shirt. "Thanks for seeing this with me."

"No problem, buddy," Jake put his hand on Nick's shoulder. "Hey, stay here for a second. I'll go get our snacks." before walking over to the concessions.

"Hi, Nick, I'm Leah. You ready to go see a movie with me?" she leaned down, extending her hand.

"Sure, it will be fun," Nick said with a slight lisp from his missing front tooth.

Bonnie, Natalie, and the older boys headed down the hall to the theater for Sister Act, as the previews had already started.

Nick stared at Jake and then at Leah with a bright, nervous expression on his face.

Leah noticed the boy's bashfulness. "Alright, what got you so quiet."

He blushed. "You're even prettier than Jake and my brother were saying you were."

This made Leah blush a little too. "Really, now. When were they saying this?"

"The other day, just us boys were hanging out. Matt said you were really pretty and that your accent was..." and he stopped, looking down, seeming to stare at a hole in the carpet.

"What did he say about my accent?" Leah kneeled down, facing the little boy. "It's okay. I won't get mad."

Nick's face flushed red, as he remade eye contact. "Matty said it was hot. And Jake said you were...a total fox."

"What did I say?" asked Jake, walking up, concerned about what the young boy was spilling to Leah.

"Nothing for you to worry about," Leah snarked, as she took Nick's hand, turning so Jake couldn't hear, "Thank you for

They Say It's a River 183

Chapter Thirty-Three

your compliment. I really appreciate it." Her mouth formed a smile toward Jake so sweetly-smug it could melt butter, enjoying the moment.

Jake's mind raced as he wondered what-in-blazes his cousin had been telling her.

Nick filled with pride, "You're welcome. Ready to see the movie?"

"Yes, have you seen it?" she asked him.

"No," Nick looked up at her as they found their seats. "My mom and dad went with Aunt Evelyn and Uncle Ron. I've wanted to."

Jake followed them, balancing a drink caddy and some popcorn.

Leah took a seat and, still holding Nick's hand, and asked, "Would you like to sit next to me since I'm so pretty?"

"Yes." Nick climbed into the seat next to her, blushing as he adjusted the seat.

"That way, if you get scared, you have both me and Jake on either side of you," Leah caught Jake's eye as the lights dimmed. Jake leaned back in his seat, trying to clear the swirl in his mind and watch the trailers.

As eerie music and a lion filled the screen, Nick whispered, "This looks scary," and then suddenly a genie with Robin Williams' voice filled the screen.

Soon the Aladdin trailer ended and the orchestral score started. They were transported to provincial France and caught up in the rapture of the film. As the film built to the scene where the Beast traps Belle in the castle, unleashing his wrath on the screen, Nick curled up to Leah and she put her arm around him for the scene. As the movie continued, they laughed, awed, and even sang along quietly to the songs they had heard before.

Midway through, the orchestra began to swell and Nick sleepily leaned against Leah. She put her arm around the little boy again. Jake looked over and saw Leah singing along, whispering the words. He lowered his hand and lightly brushed hers. She was startled from her trance of the movie and saw Jake's hand awkwardly reaching toward hers. Leah rolled her

Into the Fire

eyes and had a mild inner-debate before she opened her hand and took his into hers as they were taken in with Belle finding the love buried deep within the heart of the beast.

As the credits began to roll and young Nick began to stir, Leah let go of Jake's hand and they gathered their trash together. Nick stretched, rubbing the sleep out of his eyes, "I liked that." He reached for Leah's hand as they exited the theater, "Thanks for seeing that with me."

"You're welcome, Nicky."

"What are you grinning at, Farmer Tan?" Leah inquired about the goofy look on Jake's face.

"Nothing," was all Jake answered as they headed out into the atrium. They killed a few minutes by playing Final Lap in the arcade, with Jake and Leah switching off who had Nick help them drive.

Soon, the rest of the group left Sister Act and there was a bunch of group-talk as they walked out, into the mall. Natalie mentioned that she still had money for ice cream if anyone wanted some. The boys pleaded with Jake, who relented, and the small caravan made its way over to Kopps in Brookfield.

As they stood in line, Leah was curious. "So, it's not ice cream?"

"No," said Bonnie. "It's custard. It makes it better."

The options were Vanilla, Swiss Chocolate, and the Flavor of the Day, which was Strawberry.

The boys got a mix of Swiss Chocolate and Vanilla, Jake got Vanilla, Bonnie got Swiss Chocolate, and Leah got Strawberry.

"So, what do you think?" asked Natalie.

"It's pretty good. It tastes different, but a good difference," Leah answered in between her spoonfuls of strawberry pieces and custard.

As they finished their custard and got ready to head out for the afternoon, Leah walked to Nick, who was sitting with boys at a picnic table, "Nicky, I want to say thank you for being my movie date today." She winked at Jake.

"You're welcome," he said as she gave him a hug, Nick

Chapter Thirty-Three

giving his brother a look as if he was ten-feet tall. Matthew's jaw dropped low enough, it could have broken the pavement.

"Thank you for meeting up with us," Jake caught Bonnie's eye with a look of appreciation.

"Thanks for joining me for Sister Act so the boys could sit where they wanted and I could have some girl talk," Natalie looked toward Bonnie.

"You are always welcome to chat," Bonnie waved as they got ready to leave.

"See you later, FT," said Leah.

"Yeah, I'll," Jakee gave a half-hand wave. "I'll call you later."

"You do that," Leah replied as Bonnie laughed at his goofiness.

"Maybe you'll be up for a better walk?"

"Don't push it."

As the girls walked to their car and Natalie sent the boys to go get cleaned up from the dessert, Nick looked at Jake, "I like Leah. She's really nice."

"That, she is," Jake agreed, watching them leave.

"And I think she likes you, too," said Nick.

"Why would you say that?" asked Jake, a little curious.

"Cause she let you hold her hand the whole movie," said Nick, grinning. "Don't worry, I won't tell Natalie."

"Thanks, let's keep that our secret," said Jake as he started up the car. The rest of them walked over, ready to head home.

Chapter Thirty-Four
Long December

She clutched her cane almost as tightly as she held his hand that warm Thursday morning. As the breeze spoke between them in the silence, Edith held the same repose she'd kept since he had picked her up that morning, having said little other than the destination. She adjusted her posture and pulled Jake's hand so he could see her face more fully.

"I never knew her," her voice barely above a whisper. Her attention shifted back to the stone that had the outline of a five-petal rose etched into the marble slate and the words written: *Rosalind Key Glass - 1859 - 1897 The Rose*

Edith cleared her throat. "It was hot, that August day. Dr. Schafer came downstairs and told father that he had himself a brand new baby girl, to which all the family who had gathered clapped and gave congratulations. But the doctor raised his hand, saying he needed to talk to Bo, privately, outside.

"There, looking over the fields, he told father that there was a lot of blood with the placenta and he was concerned about the level of bleeding post-delivery. He sent his assistant to go into the city to find Dr. Fisk, who was better in these matters, to ask that he visit the house for a second opinion.

"Father spent the afternoon with me, as momma rested. Dr. Fisk came that evening and prescribed what he could and promised he would be back in the morning. Momma held me that night with the rotational attendance of the nurse and my oldest sister, Elizabeth.

"It dragged into the next day with the doctor returning in the morning and her being given transfusions, which didn't help

Chapter Thirty-Four

much at all, I've been told. Dr. Fisk, father, and mother spent the morning upstairs. Father took lunch privately with her. That afternoon, the family was called together in the master bedroom. Father by her side, she took me into her arms, clutched me close, and wept.

"She then spent time with her sister, who had come up from Chicago, and other family. Then she called each of the children to her, starting with Rhoda, Paul, and then little Alice–your great-grandmother–as they said their last goodbyes and held their mother. At this time, father dismissed everyone from the room except himself, momma, and Lizzie.

"Momma sat up in her bed and asked Lizzie to sit beside her with father. Momma cradled me in her arms and rocked me to sleep.

"She told her, 'Lizzie, as you heard from the doctor, my time is running short, and I need you to promise me before I go.'

"'What can I promise to you, momma?' she placed her hands with my mother's.

"'I want you to promise to take Edith as your own and, from this day forward, to no longer be as your sister, but to take her as your own daughter, to love and protect as you would your own.' Momma struggled to sit up as she pulled her hand to her own heart.

"Lizzie held momma's hand and promised that she would, from that day forward, take me and raise me as her own child. And she took me from momma's arms and held me.

"After momma had rested, the family gathered one last time as the doctor said she would probably pass that night," Edith said.

Her hands began to tremble. "Jacob, Can you help me sit? I need to rest."

Jake nodded and eased her back into the wheelchair, where she sat, taking in the graves surrounding them, and composed herself.

Edith wiped her eyes, took a breath as she shared her heart. "Family came and went in the hours that followed. As she held my father's hand, Alice remembered her telling him to 'Be the strength that I will never be.'

"As the time began to draw near, she called to Lizzie, 'May I hold her one last time?' Lizzie came with me and sat by her on the bed. She kissed me and kissed my father and held his hand 'til she faded from us. Her last words were, 'I will see you soon, my love,' and passed that night. And so she was laid to rest where we are now.

"Alice told me, years later, that the sorrow of that moment seared her heart with a wound that would never quite heal. In a way, she said it steeled her heart for when we lost Paul at the Battle of Belleau Wood. That day, I came into the care of my older sister, and she became my wet nurse, as Solomon was just a little over a year at the time and—"

"Aunt Edith," Jake interrupted. "Great Uncle Solomon, I'm confused. He was like our second cousin or something whose parents died, dad always said. He moved to Minnesota and his family still lives there, cause I visited them in eighty-nine, but—"

Edith stopped him, "To the world, yes, he was a child that we took in within the family, whose parents had died in a train accident, and Lizzie stayed in Marinette until he was of strength to travel that Summer, which shows my mother's influence on the situation. But the truth is a secret long-sealed past her death,"Edith pointed to her sister's grave, not far from them. "Because Solomon was her child.'"

Chapter Thirty-Five
Show Me the Way

"Wait," Jake was shocked, "He was?"

"Yes, he was. Elizabeth and Daddy had a falling out in the summer of 1894 and she ran off. It broke Momma's heart and she didn't speak to Father for three months after she left. She came back a year later, six months along, and Momma arranged for her to stay with extended family up near Canada. The winter Solomon was born, there was a bad train accident and two of Mother's extended family were killed. The doctor was a friend and the birth certificate read the names of a family member who had passed. Momma made sure the legal arrangements declared her guardianship of Solomon."

"How did she pull that off?" Jake wondered.

"Though my mother had married a Glass, she was, always and forever, a Key. The Keys were a powerful and progressive family. I am curious, as you visited Solomon's daughter and her family out near Minneapolis. Did you have any questions after the visit?"

"Several," Jacob remembered the visit and the conversations afterward. "But I wasn't sure how to ask. I remember trying to find pictures of Solomon when we got back and I couldn't find any, except one in an old album dated '1922', and you were in it, Aunt Edith."

"And?"

"Solomon was black. I asked Dad about it and he sharply asked me if I had a problem with it. I said 'no' and that was the end of it. He said Solomon had been adopted into the family and family was family."

Edith continued, "So, I lived in the house with Lizzie and

Show Me the Way

Solomon until Father found a small house and set Lizzie up for a place of her own. A few years after that, she met Neil Connor and they married and she had Laura, Carrie, and Emmit."

"Grandpa Alvin once said that Solomon was one of the kindest people he had ever met."

"Yes, he was, and he and I were thick-as-thieves growing up. He was accepted, for the time, within our family and, thankfully, within our community. He was my defender, even when I deserved the trouble my mouth got me into. He had the warmest smile and his eyes were so bright and similar to yours. To let anyone wonder, he truly was a Glass."

"Why is that?"

Edith's eyes sparkled. "Because he had gray eyes, just like you."

"Wow," said Jake.

"Lizzie became my mother in all respects and Solomon and I kind of had our own lives. Her children with Connor were all seven or more years younger than us. I got along okay with Neil, but Solomon and he clashed as Solomon became a young adult. Lizzie said her heart broke a second time when he went to Minnesota. She would visit him whenever she could."

Jake sat quietly as he stared at the grave of his great-great-grandmother and examined the engraving.

"The Rose, was that her nickname?" he asked.

"Yes," said Edith, "She was the Rose."

"But why isn't there a rose on her gravestone?"

"But there is, Jacob. Have you ever seen a wild rose? Come, let's get back in the car. I could use some air conditioning."

As they drove, she had him head to a local community garden she knew. He helped her out and she had him wheel her to a section with prairie roses in whites, reds, and pinks. As he pushed her through the gardens, Edith pointed out other plants. They talked and enjoyed the afternoon.

They returned to the manor, where he joined her in her room, sitting in a chair. She made herself comfortable sitting on the bed, the emotional toll of reliving the past and the heat of the day catching up with her.

Chapter Thirty-Five

"Jacob, in the drawer to the left, there is a velvet bag. Could you grab it for me?"

Jacob went to the mahogany roll-top desk and eased open the creaking drawer. He found the velvet pouch under some legal folders and handed it to Edith.

She opened it and pulled out a weathered yellow parchment.

"Before I was born, my mother shared with father that she had decided to pass her family line of the Rose to me."

"What is the line of the Rose?" Jake felt like the surprises about his family had reached their limit already for the day.

"Within the Key family, there has been a generational tradition of giving a certain rose name and a blessing of the Rose to one child each generation. My aunt, Patricia, told me the tradition dated back to at least the fifteen-hundreds. My mother, before she died, had my father write a note letting me know I was the carrier of the line. The letter was sealed and given to me by my father on my eighteenth birthday."

"As you know, Jacob, I've never had any children who lived into full adulthood. My Rose was also a flower that faded far too soon," her words bitter at the memory. Jake's heart ached as he held her hand.

"I have had many years to think and choose who I should give my gift to–who will keep the line alive. Jacob, I have chosen you, which is why I asked Alvin for you to help me this summer. So I could give you that gift, to take it with you and share it with your children, and your children's children." She handed him the velvet bag and gave him a hug, "I've always cared for you, Jacob. You've always taken time with me over the years and, even when you were little, you would come and spend the afternoons with your grandfather at the Jennings Park house. What sealed my decision was watching you with Darla. That truly showed your heart. Most of your cousins treat her differently or are unsure how to be with her. You didn't. You accepted and loved her as she was with all of yourself. So, within your heart is a rose that I hope you find to give." She leaned toward Jacob as he leaned in and she kissed his cheek and hugged him. After their goodbyes,

Show Me the Way

he headed out to the Oldsmobile and into the afternoon.

Jake was torn within himself as he sorted through all that he had heard. He didn't want to go back to the house. He turned onto 167, heading toward the lake. He reached the dirt turnoff, pulling past a small grove of trees, and followed them to a small parking lot, empty that afternoon. He parked the car and headed past the small trails until he reached a park bench that looked out over the expanse of Lake Michigan.

He fished the purple velvet pouch Edith had given him out of his pocket, unzipped it, and his heart stopped. Folded within the yellow parchment was the rose.

Jake carefully placed the brooch back into the pouch and unfolded the letter.

> My dearest Edith,
>
> I love you with all my heart, but fate has seen to it that my life must be exchanged for your own into this world. I know there will be times you will look back on this day with questions this world can never answer, but I beg you not to look at this day in anger. Though you shall never see me in this life, may you feel my love within your spirit, and may it grow within your heart as you blossom into the beautiful woman you will become. I give you the promise of the Rose, for I was the first to carry it in this new world. May you find within your line the one to keep it. I give this from my heart as a promise to know that you are not forgotten, and I in turn will live on in your heart and in the hearts of those who carry the name.
>
> With all my love in life and in death,
> Rosalind Key Glass
> August 20, 1897

Jake folded the letter and nestled it into the pouch next to the silver rose and wondered. *Who am I,* he thought, *to be the one...?* He struggled within his heart and mind, wrestling with who he would be. How the choices, even now, shaped where he would go. This made a difference; now he carried something

Chapter Thirty-Five

greater. A promise to keep to those of the past and the assurance that the line would be carried forward–that they would live on in the hearts and lives of those who carried the name.

On the drive back to the cottage the radio was off, his thoughts providing more than noise for his ears. Grabbing some worms from the fridge, he rowed out onto the lake and watched the sunset while he fished, lost in his thoughts, before going back into the cottage to get some rest. The fits of a restless mind finally gave in to the sleep his body was fighting for.

Yet in the night, Jake felt a boat's rhythm beneath him, gliding through a haze in time as he drifted on the water. The voice of a little girl snapped his focus to the present, or what seemed to be.

"Daddy, what are you looking at?" the voice echoed, small and familiar. He turned, surprised to see not one, but two young girls in the boat with him.

"I'm...not sure," he murmured, looking around toward a pier, slowly coming into focus. There, in front of a weathered green cottage, was a girl walking on the oak pier, her long dark hair floating behind her, delicate and out of place. Shadows fell around her, twisting in the light, obscuring her figure, then bringing her back again. Her face flickered like an old movie reel stuck between frames.

Jake tried to get a better look, his heart racing with a sense of recognition. The shadows parted for a moment, and he saw her: Leah, just as she had been this summer, her familiar features reaching out to him across some unbridgeable distance.

Another voice wafted behind him in the boat, snapping him back. "Daddy, isn't that the cottage you stayed at when you were young?"

He nodded, half-awake in the dream, half-rooted in this hazy future, trying to keep his daughters–his daughters?–safe and steady on the boat as he maneuvered back toward the cottage.

The boat finally reached the dock and Jake caught his breath, turning to the girls to speak when the older asked, "Who is she?"

"Who?" Jake wondered aloud as she moved her hand

Show Me the Way

and pointed to the dock behind.

Jake felt every pulse of his heart as he turned, because there, standing on the pier, was the young girl. The haunting familiarity took his breath away. He felt his world lurch, the boat rocking, the dream slipping as her face blurred into shadow once more, and through the fog her hand reached out for his. He leaned over the bow, reaching toward her, his gaze locking onto those eyes–his own–gray and piercing, staring back at him through her face. But the boat began to rock further, and he heard a voice call, "Daddy," from behind him as he felt himself slip. Her eyes pierced his soul until he hit the water with a splash, breathless, disoriented, caught somewhere between what was real and what had only just vanished. He thrashed against the murky deep, till the pain of striking wood jarred him awake, as he now lay on the floor beside the bed.

Chapter Thirty-Six
Save the Best for Last

Leah looked at the clock. Just past one, perfect, she thought. "Hey Bonnie."

"Yes," came her call back from the grill.

"What time are your cousins getting here? It should be any minute now. Why?"

"I was wondering if I can head out after this?"

"Head out? Where?" Bonnie put down the spatula and looked at her cousin.

"I was thinking I could stop by and see if our *friend* needed any help with painting."

"I'm sure he'd take it," Bonnie narrowed her eyes, rolling the spatula in her hand. "Just don't leave me hanging."

"I won't," Leah replied, taking a few minutes to tidy up and restock cups and lids before the cousins rolled in.

Twenty minutes later, Leah headed down the dirt road behind the diner. Stopping by Clara's, she took a few minutes to change into a clean t-shirt and shorts before walking up the road toward the green cottage. On the side of the house, lost in his own world with headphones on and a discman sticking out of the side pocket on his carpenter jeans, Jake leaned against the rigged ladder, painting the window trim.

Leah waited until he was coming down the ladder to get his attention, "Would you like some help?"

Jake almost jumped out of his skin and spun around at the base of the ladder.

"Oh, hey, Leah. Sure, I don't want you to mess up your clothes. This green paint gets on everything," Jake motioned to the spattered clothing.

"I figured I could help you with some trim work," she

offered.

"Sure." Jake fished out a small paint bucket and a trim brush.

"How much more are you planning to do this afternoon?"

"I was gonna try to at least get this side done, then I'm cleaning up for the day. How about you?"

"Just finished my morning shift at the diner. Bonnie is running some deliveries for Clara this afternoon."

"I appreciate the help if you have time for it," Jake set his refilled paint tray up on the scaffolding and went back up the ladder.

An hour later, with the windows and lower lattice trimmed and the side painted with a fresh coat, Leah and Jake sat for a minute before cleaning up for the day.

"Thanks for helping me knock that out," Jake extended a paint rag to her. "Saved me a good hour or more."

"No problem," Leah replied, taking the rag and wiping off a few of the flecks that decorated her hands.

"You've done this before," Jake admired the clean lines on the lattice.

"A little," she chuckled. "My family has had enough work projects over the years. This is just another one." She tapped down the paint can on the lid and washed out the brushes.

Back in the house, Jake rinsed his hands and looked at the green coating on his clothes. "Hey, I'm gonna go upstairs real quick and get changed. Feel free to get yourself something to drink." He pointed to the kitchen as he headed upstairs.

Leah got a glass of tea and walked out to the screened-in porch and looked out toward the lake, relaxing on the couch as she waited. The bustle of the lake was starting to pick up for the afternoon.

When Jake came back downstairs, his stomach was rumbling. "Want to take the canoe out to Swenson's for a picnic?"

"Not a bad idea, it's a nice enough day." She helped him load food and drinks into the cooler and they made their way to the boathouse.

"So, Leah," said Jake. "Now that we actually get a few

Chapter Thirty-Six

minutes, just us, what's your story? Everyone hints about it, but I'm curious to hear it from you."

"Nothing that unusual," Leah shrugged. "I grew up in Lilburn, GA, in a red brick split-level, tucked away under the shade of loblolly pines. Some of my earliest memories are walking along the rolling hills near Camp Creek and dipping my feet into its chilly waters. My whole self felt wrapped in her arms as we sat along its banks, taking in the potpourri of the oconees, the rolling stream, and that soft vanilla that seemed ever-present with her.

"My dad worked for Southern Energy, and my mom worked in administration at Georgia Tech's computer science department. They met at Georgia Tech during their sophomore year when my dad needed a math tutor, and my mom was assigned to help him. He used to joke that he didn't let his grades improve too much until they were officially dating, for fear she wouldn't think he needed a tutor anymore."

"My parents met in college too." Jake looked up while digging through a pile of rigging and flotation devices for paddles in the boathouse. "What were your friends like?"

"Denise and I have been getting into trouble for as long as I can remember. Her mother worked with my mom at the university and lived nearby. Our little group included Candice and Grace from school. We took a chance on letting my dad's friend's son join us, even though he was a boy. But Stewart was a good balance for our party of five.

"So you weren't all prissy and tea parties?" Jake tossed the now-found paddles and life jackets on the ground next to the cooler chest.

"Denise and Grace had older brothers, so they were a little tomboyish. We spent our days crashing through woods and streams, normally ending up at different people's houses as we traveled around. Our summers included playing softball, which is how we all got to know Yolanda. She moved in the summer before sixth grade when her dad came to work for the Braves. She introduced me to the world of Major League Baseball, and I've been hooked ever since. What about you?"

Save the Best for Last

"Stanford is where my parents' stars crossed, which should answer a few questions you've heard discussed. My dad grew up out here, and my mom's family has lived in Arizona since after World War II. They became quite the power couple after graduation, helping my grandpa expand the mining company." Jake headed back into the boathouse. "Can you give me a hand?" He opened the door and began moving the canoe out onto the grass. After a few minutes, the awkward dance was complete, and the canoe rested on the ground.

"My Aunt Tanya babysat me and her friend's son while our parents were at work when I wasn't at my grandma's. That's how I met Allen. It was pretty much just us in school, along with Laura, who lived two houses down until midway through first grade. One day, I missed school because of a trip or something. When I came back, there was a girl with black hair sitting across from me. She didn't talk to anyone, and at lunch, she was all by herself. Laura and I walked over and invited her to sit with us. She thanked us and told me her name was Marta."

"And the plot thickens." Amusement filled Leah's face as she sat on the cooler chest.

"I thought she was weird because she was always staring at me. One day, I finally asked her why, and she said, 'Because of your eyes. I've never seen ones like them before.' I blushed and told her my grandpa had eyes like mine. Then there was the day her jeans snagged on the merry-go-round, and she fell, getting dragged along the ground. She tore her hand open, and there was blood everywhere. The other kids were running and screaming. I took off my shirt and used it as a bandage, as Allen's mom had taught us to do first aid. I stayed with her and the teachers until the ambulance arrived, then went with her and her mom to the hospital."

"Oh my gosh, you weren't making that up."

"God's honest truth. She had a large D-shaped scar after that. We were the closest of friends until her family moved to Phoenix. The moms threw a going-away party for the family, and we sat the whole time, hand in hand. For the last goodbye, she kissed my cheek and whispered, 'Someday I will see you

Chapter Thirty-Six

again. Don't forget me, okay?'"

"And, let me guess, you forgot?" Leah feigned shock.

"Funny, I figured she was your first kiss."

"Nope. We wrote a little bit, but not much past fifth grade. Fall of seventh grade, Susan and I started hanging out more, but I guess you could say she was my first girlfriend. And my first—"

"Wait, is there a different Susan?" Leah interrupted, confused. "Your friend Curtis' girlfriend is named Susan, from what you and Bonnie were talking about."

"Yes, one and the same."

"So, how did that happen?" Leah was bemused.

"She was part of the group with Laura," Jake explained. "I was starting to play the guitar, and she could play the keyboard."

"Okay," Leah leaned in. "Do you have pictures of any of these people?"

Jake got out his wallet and showed her a spring picture of him, Allen, Laura, Curtis, and Susan.

"She the blonde?"

"No, that's Laura. That's her there, on the end."

"Hmm." Leah studied the girl with long black hair.

"And what about Marta? I'm sure you have a few of her."

"Here," He flipped through and showed her a picture of a striking Hispanic girl with wavy black hair and fiery brown eyes.

"You know, Farmer Tan, I think you've got a type."

"What are you talking about?" Jake was confused.

"Susan's Filipino, loves rock music, *Star Trek,* and *Doctor Who.* Marta is Hispanic and Miss Homecoming Princess."

"Never mind," Leah shook her head.

Jake tossed his sandals into the canoe and placed the cooler inside as they slid the boat down into the shallow water. Jake steadied the boat while Leah climbed into the front. He pushed off in the shallow water, stepping into the boat and using his paddle to propel them as they glided out into the lake.

"Where do you want to head to?" Leah looked back at him.

"Let's stay along the east shore as we head to the

Save the Best for Last

Swenson's," Jake pointed to the right.

They glided through the water, passing assorted docks and painted boathouses.

"So, back to your first kiss?" Leah asked, curious about where this was going.

"Around late fall of seventh grade, I knew Susan had a crush on me because Laura had hinted at it. We started the classic sitting-together-at-lunch routine and hanging out. That Christmas, I got her a little stuffed Santa frog and asked her if she would go with me to a New Year's party at La Paloma with my family. She said yes, and so we started 'going out.'"

"Whatever that means in seventh grade," Leah laughed.

"Then Valentine's Day came and she wrote 'I ♥ you' in my valentine. A few weeks later, we went hiking with some families up in Sabino Canyon. We hiked past the falls and sat on one of the ridges that looked out over the city.

"As we talked, it started to get near sunset. She looked out and said, 'It is so beautiful up here.' Not missing a beat and channeling my best Alex P. Keaton, I answered, 'Almost as beautiful as you.' When I looked back at her, she was leaning in. I wasn't sure what to do, so I leaned in too but bumped her face and started to kiss her cheek. She turned her head and kissed me on the lips. I was so surprised I started to say something, but she stopped me and said, 'Just kiss me.' So I did.

"We got back to the paved road at dusk and met up with the parents' group. My mom was less-than-thrilled, but that's how it started."

"Oh my gosh, you are such a nerd," Leah rolled her eyes.

"Oh, you have no idea. Casanova, I am not," Jake ran his hand along the top of the water as they coasted by a family of ducks.

"I could have told you that," Leah shot him a look.

"Ouch!" Jake rubbed an imaginary sting. "Whatever that was, it lasted until about late May–it wasn't much–and I left for Wisconsin. I was gone for almost three months, and by the time I got back, Curtis had moved into their home off of Prince, which was near Susan's. And, well, so it goes."

"So, how about you?" Jake asked as they turned out

Chapter Thirty-Six

toward the open water, heading back to the little beach. "Who was your first kiss?"

"Stewart," Leah began. "He was the brother I never had. He was my defender and my voice of reason when I was about to hurt myself. We never really went out or anything, but I never really saw anybody else, and neither did he," Leah remembered wistfully.

"I found out long after, from Denise, that everyone assumed we were together, and she never questioned it because we acted like a couple. He would hold my hand and I would hold his, but it never really felt like much until around eighth grade. I guess I started to look at him differently. I wasn't sure if he would feel the same, but we did care a lot for each other," Leah's mind lingered in days long past.

"Then the school year finished, and we were all excited about going on to high school. One hot June afternoon, Stewart called, his voice broken, and asked if he could come over. He told me over cookies my mom had made that his dad had gotten a different job. He was surprised I didn't know because my own father helped him find it. I was furious and heartbroken. At my dad, at his. Just mad at the world for taking away my friend," she spoke past the halt in her voice.

"He shared my passion for adventure and we explored all the world we could reach with our bikes that summer. That August, before they had to move to Fayetteville, we had a cookout at Tribble Mill with family and friends. That afternoon, we took a walk around the lake as we reminisced about all that we had done over the years and the fun we'd had there, canoeing, hiking, and more.

"We followed the eastern loop trail and rested on boulders overlooking the lake. Stewart was talking about all the cool things he still wanted to do, worried he wouldn't get a chance now. He questioned if he'd be good enough for cross-country or if he'd make friends. I saw the fear that engulfed him and my heart ached. Then he asked, 'What are you afraid of missing out on?' I looked at those emerald eyes, weary and red, and brushed his wet cheek with my hand. 'This,' was all that came out as I touched his face and kissed him. He held me tight and wiped away the tears I spilled," she sat in silence as her heart pulled back to that moment.

"We rejoined the group and Denise cornered me, asking, 'So, what happened?' I played dumb, but she wouldn't have it. So, I told her. She said she could tell something was different. I kept quiet on it, worried my mom would freak out–and rightfully so!"

"Did she find out?"

"Of course. That boy couldn't keep his mouth shut to save his life. He told his dad, who, of course, told mine, and, let's just say Mom went all sappy over it."

"So, where is that now?"

"We kept in touch. He was amazing in cross country. He and my dad still catch up sometimes and that's when I see him."

As they glided into the bay, Leah took off her sandals and stepped out of the boat into the shallow water. Jake hopped out, dragging the canoe until it was beached on the sand. They each took a handle and settled the cooler onto the picnic table.

"So, we've got some cold cuts and cheese, an apple, and a peach for you, Miss Georgia," he said with a smile as he prepared the spread. "And whatever's in that container you brought."

"Banana pudding," she revealed, quite proud of her find. "You still had some in the fridge."

"That stuff is the bomb."

"It is," Leah agreed.

As they finished lunch, enjoying the cool breeze off the lake, Jake looked at Leah as her hair drifted in around her face. "Thanks for hanging out this afternoon, Leah. It was nice reminiscing."

"My pleasure," Leah replied, relaxing in the sun, enjoying the afternoon without bells, needy customers, or phone calls with her family.

They finished the banana pudding, and Jake noticed it was time to start heading back. They packed the food and supplies back into the cooler and reloaded the canoe.

"Leah," Jake took her hand, assisting her into the canoe,

Chapter Thirty-Six

"I guess my big question is, what's next?"

"What do you mean?" Leah froze, unsure what he was referencing as she searched his eyes. "You said you're leaving Atlanta, so what's going on with that?"

"I'm still struggling with it," Leah admitted. "I don't really want to go to Houston, you know? Starting over sucks."

"It does. Still wondering what I'm gonna do, too." He stepped in behind her, pushing the boat into the deeper water with the oar. "Do you know anyone out there?"

"Well, just my grandparents and my aunt and her family. I really don't like them—my aunt and cousins, I mean. I know that sounds terrible, but she thinks she's my mom now and is pulling every string with all her might."

"And you're just going with it?" Jake struggled to believe the strong will he had encountered in her so far had given up without a fight.

"No. I made my dad promise me that we will live in Baytown, not Tomball."

"So, is that a big difference?" Jake questioned, having never been to Houston.

"It'd be like if I lived in Madison compared with where Bonnie lives."

"Oh, enough distance to have space in day-to-day life, but not like you live on the moon," Jake chuckled.

"Exactly," Leah remarked.

They stayed close to the eastern shoreline on their way back, the arrival of the lake's weekenders increasing on the open water. Jake brought his thoughts back to where they had been earlier in the day.

"How much longer are you here for?"

"I fly back on July fifth, a little over two weeks. Why?" she asked, looking back over her shoulder at Jake.

"Because, I..." He thought about how to best say it. "I enjoy spending time with you, Leah."

Leah felt a brush against her heart as she replied, "So do I. I'm glad you're here this summer."

Jake angled the canoe as it glided along the pier, mooring

it securely to a post. He set the cooler chest down by the back porch and took in his view of her in the afternoon sun. "I wish we had more than two weeks."

"And why is that, Farmer Tan?" She studied him, sitting beside him on the step.

"Because, with you, I feel something different. I can't explain it." He felt drawn into her blue eyes, the dream from the night before still as fresh as the paint on the trim within his thoughts. "This is gonna sound bizarre, but I feel our meeting wasn't an accident." He touched her hand as he spoke. "Do you know what I mean?"

His eyes searched deeper into her heart than she was ready for. She took his hand as she peered back into his own.

"Jacob," she curled his fingers within hers. "Far more than you know."

Chapter Thirty-Seven
I Can't Make You Love Me

Jake pulled back up to the cottage after dropping Leah off. His heart was still a tangle of emotions. Inside the cottage, he pulled out the jewelry bag that he had gotten from Edith. He held the brooch between his fingers, his thoughts lost within it as he crossed the room. The light flashing on the answering machine caught his attention. Clicking the play button, he heard Lucy's voice crackle on the recording.

"Hi, Jacob. I wanted to call and remind you that we will all be out at the cottage Sunday after church, so if you need to clean up before we come out, please do so. Oh, and Marta called this afternoon, looking for you. She was sweet, as always, and asked if you could give her a call. I have thoughts on that, but your grandfather is here, so I'll save them for now. Love you and see you soon. Bye."

Jake stared at the recorder, wondering why Marta was calling. She had called in years past, but why now? He carefully placed the rose on the table and dialed a number he knew by heart.

The phone buzzed three times until a stout voice snapped in his ear, "Hola."

"Hi Hector," Jake tried not to sound nervous when he talked to her oldest brother, who had never quite liked him. "Is Marta there?"

"Perdedor," he mumbled coldly, then yelled, "Marta, tu novio imbécil está hablando por teléfono."

"Él no es mi novio," Marta's voice carried in the background as she grabbed the phone. "Hey, Jake, thanks for calling back."

"Sure, just a little surprised you called."

I Can't Make You Love Me

"You know, just wondering how your summer is going? You and the girls having fun?" Her soft words decorating the bait with care through the phone..

Jake growled within himself, exhaling to control his temper. This had the overarching stench of his mother. The chess pieces were in play. Jake calculated how much he wanted to say and what message he wanted to send. "The girls?" The words rolled off his tongue as confused as he could make them. He let her fill him in on the source of this search party.

"Your friends up there, Kristen or Bridget, I can never remember," her sass dripped through the phone. "My mom saw Cindy the other day at Dillard's and they got to talking. Apparently, you've found some fun in lake country again," the sauciness sharpened to a verbal sword. "The farm girl isn't enough, you had to go after her cousin, too."

"What are you getting at, Marta?" Jake's tone was crisp through each word as he gripped the receiver. "As I recall, you were the one who pushed us to break up."

"Yes, I guess I did, because I wasn't enough to compete with your true love," her cold words continued. "Matt, I've discovered, seems to suffer from the same affliction," she added with a touch of resignation.

"Oh, your tee times can't compete with travel ball?" Jake added dryly.

"Like you'd know," Marta brushed his remark aside. "I will say it was nice for a while, to be with someone who desired to spend time just being with me and hear my heart and not just try to 'feel my soul'," her disgust seeping in.

He shook off the slap. "So, why are you calling me?" "Because, Rye," her voice softened. "In three weeks, you're home, and our senior year is alive in living color. And I don't want us to throw away everything we've had over these years. I mean, we found each other again, and we thought it was over, and I've..." She got quiet.

"You've what?" his voice dismissing the games.

"I've been missing you," the words slid through the phone with a bitter hurt. "Haven't you?"

Chapter Thirty-Seven

Jacob felt the frustration in his heart of conversations he had heard before. "Haven't I what?"

"Missed me?" came the questioning voice, waiting for a presupposed answer.

Jake picked up the rose off the table and rolled it in his hand. "Marta, I...I don't know," he said, getting quiet.

Pain was all that answered. "Jacob, are you serious? You really don't? What about our weekends at Peppersauce?" She choked up. "After...everything, you're done?"

"From going back to like before?" he questioned "Yes. If I've learned anything in the last four years, it's that reliving the same life and expecting something different from it really is insanity. And I don't want to do that anymore."

"I hate you," sliced through the phone, aimed for his heart.

"I don't." Jake stood and walked toward the screened porch and felt the breeze off the lake. "But I've changed in that time and so have you." Jake stopped and thought about how to say what he really wanted to tell her for so long. "Honestly—"

"Honestly, what?" her voice was distant.

"You deserve better." Jake realized the truth in the words. "What I'm about to do and the path I'm about to take isn't one you should have to follow."

"You're really giving up Stanford?" came her hollow question.

"Yes," he answered knowing the dominoes this would push.

"Wow."

"And that's not fair to you, as you aced your college interviews and probably gonna get a scholarship somewhere here soon," Jake swallowed.

"It still hurts," she whispered.

"I know." His words filled from the depths of his heart, "I know."

Neither spoke, the weight of what they couldn't say left in the silence until Jake's voice broke in with a hesitant goodbye. "I need to get to things here. I'll call you when I get back. Okay?

I Can't Make You Love Me

I hope you have a good rest of the summer."

"Thanks," her response was shaky. "You too." She broke into a more urgent tone, "You know your mom is gonna totally cut you off, right? You're gonna throw your life away."

"No," Jake cradled the rose within his hand. "I'm going to find it."

Chapter Thirty-Eight
One

"Where are we going exactly?" Leah asked in her half awake state. Her eyes glazed, watching the bramble of trees and brush separating the houses roll by with interspaced views of Lake Michigan. The ride had been pretty quiet since Jake had picked her up at around 9:30 that morning. The silence was only broken when Jake flipped on the radio. Leah scanned through stations till they heard the strains of Nirvana coming through the speakers from the Marquette campus station as they pulled out onto Highway 43, heading north. Downtown Milwaukee faded behind them as they drove and late-June's pleasant morning weather accompanied them until they got off around Whitefish Bay and headed along Lakeshore Drive.

Jake rolled his window down to enjoy the fresh morning air. The smell of the lake and trees brought Leah back to the present.

"You'll see here in a minute," he answered. They turned onto a little two-lane road and passed a sign for East Bay Gorge. As they pulled into the small parking lot, Leah got out and stretched while Jake glanced at the information board highlighting the trails.

They strolled along the winding path, the light breeze blowing Leah's hair around her. At the top of a ridge, the trees parted to reveal an expansive view of Lake Michigan.

As the wind off the lake whistled by them, Jake motioned toward the water. "I know it's not the ocean, but it's as close as I can get."

"I love it," Leah took his hand as they looked out at the blue meeting the horizon.

"Can I ask you something?"

One

"Sure," Leah replied, unsure of the tone in his voice as he looked out at the water.

"Why are you leaving it all? You don't have to go."

Leah's reached for the answer that few in this world understood. "I've thought about that. I don't have family there in Atlanta. My mom was born and raised in Tennessee, in a small town by the Ocoee River. My grandma and my cousins live up there, but I'd have to start all over there, too. And as much as I love my family there, they all have their agendas. I'm hoping that staying with my dad will allow me to live a little closer to how I want."

"And what is that?" Jake wondered.

"I wish I knew," she chuckled. "But I know what it's not. I don't want to live under my aunt's thumb–or my grandma's. I want to make my own decisions. I want to learn the beauty that my mom found in her life, that passion and joy that filled her. I want that and I want to find it for myself."

"What do you mean?" Jake questioned as they walked along the ridge.

"I mean, I watched my parents. They loved each other, and my mom loved me. I know I drove her crazy, but she loved me for good and bad. And my mom and dad, I didn't really notice until she got sick and then I saw how much they loved each other."

"I'm glad you had that," Jake grimaced. "My parents have had a pretty rough marriage. They love each other, but they nearly split about three-and-a-half years ago because of everything going on."

"Really? I mean, I've had friends whose parents have split. What was going on?" Leah saw the concern on his face.

"No one talked about it. It was like a big open secret that everyone knew, but no one would address. Kyle and I saw it, clear as day, when it would break open."

Leah wasn't following him. "Break open? What was going on?"

"My mom is an alcoholic," he whispered. Words he had struggled to admit to himself for years.

Chapter Thirty-Eight

"I'm so sorry," she pulled his hand close to her.

"Don't be sorry," Jake's eyes spoke with his words. "It's been a journey, but she's making her way out. Sober for over two years now. Before, our world was teetering on a daily hurricane. Like a dark cloud that always hung on the horizon, just needing a little push. She'd get stressed and we'd come home from school and try to ride it out. Dad traveled a lot, so sometimes when it got bad we'd stay at my grandparents'. Or if Kyle was good there, I'd go stay with friends. "

"Wow, how long had this been going on?"

"She's always struggled with it a little, I guess. But four years ago, it all came apart. Dad traveled as much as he could because when he was home, they'd fight. When he was gone, she'd drink until she passed out. Thankfully, my grandfather owned the company, so she didn't get fired, but he, along with friends and my dad and us, finally had an intervention. We told her she had to go to rehab or we'd leave," Jake stopped walking.

"It was tough. It hurt so much. She cried and asked why we didn't love her and asked me why I had turned against her," Jake shivered, reliving that day, his voice choked.

He turned away to face the waves frothing at the shoreline. Leah could see the lines running down his face as she squeezed his hand. "You did the right thing," she said quietly as the silence spoke between them.

"We did it because we loved her," his hand shaking, as he talked. "We loved her so much that we would risk being without her so she could get the help she needed."

"For the first month, Dad wouldn't let us visit her. He'd come back and just go to his room and lock his door after he was with her. Kyle would come and sleep in my bed, like he did when he was little, when Mom would drink too much."

"We eventually started to see her once every other week. She was there for nine months, and when she came back, things were rocky that first year. We all were starting over. But, thankfully, she's been sober for over two years now," Jake reached for a brighter light in his heart. "She still has her moments, and she hasn't lost her temper. But, as she tells my dad, 'Paul, every

One

day I make a choice and each day, choosing gets a little easier,'" his words were measured as he squeezed her hand.

"I can't imagine what you've gone through," she pulled him with her as she walked down the slope toward the beach. Jacob saw the clouds rolling in and wondered if they should head back.

"But we got through it, we are still together," Jake told her. "I mean, you lost your mom and you've still got it together. I'd be a wreck."

She didn't say anything as she let go of Jake's hand and walked down the hill toward the water.

"Leah, we might want to start back to the car. I think it's going to rain," he called out.

"Are you going to melt?" she teased as she reached the sand. Kicking off her shoes, she waded out into the water. She knelt down and began sifting her hands in the shallows. Jake stood in silence as he watched her diligently digging in the water until she turned around. Her eyes were red, but her smile belied her tears.

"This," she said as she walked toward Jake, holding up shiny pieces of green and purple that glinted lightly from the sun breaking through the clouded sky. "This is how."

"Sea glass?" Jake questioned as she walked up to him.

"You know where it comes from, right?"

"Yeah, discarded glass bottles and trash that got put in the lake."

"Don't you ever look for it when you're here?"

"No, but Nat's mom does. She has pieces of all different colors, but I don't get it. How does this help you?"

"I'm gonna tell you something my grandfather told me this spring when he took me out to the ocean with my dad," Leah rolled the green glass within her hand.

"Sometimes, we get broken and feel discarded and tossed out within life, just like this glass. We're scattered and churned as we struggle with all that we are dealing with, the questions in our life, the pain we face, the loneliness. But here's what he told me: that when that happens, we can find out who we really are.

Chapter Thirty-Eight

And from all the pain comes this," she held up the purple ball of glass for Jacob.

"And that was held deep inside your heart, all the pain and trouble and tears, it wasn't wasted." She placed her hand on his. "Just like that bottle was worn and shaped so you can see a beauty that you never knew."

Jacob's heart burned as he was drawn into her tear-stained eyes.

"Jacob, with you, I see that. A beauty that shines through the brokenness, just like I have found with all I've gone through. But, that's why I can smile brighter and treasure what I still have. I know that hard times are still coming, but I've been hoping and praying that I would one day find someone who could see that beauty within me, just like I see it within them, and that it would be worth it."

Jacob took the piece of sea glass and held it as if he was holding a precious jewel.

"I..." Jake's heart knew the words before his head. "I saw it from the moment I met you, that glint in your eyes. That flicker of something more. And I don't want to let it go."

They were interrupted by a thunderclap overhead and Leah jumped closer to him.

Leah took the green piece from her hand and placed it within Jake's, next to the purple jewel. She placed her hand over his as the rain began to fall.

"I've never been so afraid in my whole life but, right now, I don't care. I don't care about Texas, I don't care about the future, and I sure don't care about this rain," she laughed as the skies opened. "I only care about one thing," she placed her hand on his cheek, looking deep into his eyes.

"And what's that?" Jake pulled her close, shielding her from the wind.

"You," was all that left her mouth as she closed the distance between them. Their lips touched and the dam within their hearts broke with a torrent more powerful than the storm that raged around them.

Appendix

Eaton / Cloud Family

Georgia Side of the Family
- **Brett Eaton**, 40 years old – Son of Philip and Ethel Eaton. Was married to Lisa Cloud (deceased). Father of Leah Eaton.
- **Lisa Cloud-Eaton**, 40 years old (deceased) – Daughter of Charles and Eunice Cloud. Second cousin of Trevor Cloud. Mother of Leah Eaton.
- **Leah Eaton**, 17 years old – Daughter of Brett and Lisa Eaton. Second cousin of Bonnie Cloud.

Texas Side of the Family
- **Philip Eaton**, 73 years old – Married to Ethel Beard. Father of Brett Eaton and Caroline Eaton-Martin.
- **Ethel Beard-Eaton**, 71 years old – Married to Philip Eaton. Mother of Brett Eaton and Caroline Eaton-Martin.
- **Caroline Eaton-Martin**, 38 years old – Daughter of Philip and Ethel Eaton. Married to Jerry Martin. Sister of Brett Eaton.

Wisconsin Side of the Family
- **Harold Beck**, 68 years old – Married to Clara Swanson. Father of Karl Beck and Betty Beck-Cloud.
- **Clara Swanson-Beck**, 66 years old – Married to Harold Beck. Mother of Karl Beck and Betty Beck-Cloud.
- **Trevor Cloud**, 42 years old – Lisa Cloud's second cousin. Married to Betty Beck. Father of Bonnie and Joseph.
- **Betty Beck-Cloud**, 41 years old – Daughter of Harold and Clara. Mother of Bonnie and Joseph.
- **Bonnie Cloud**, 17 years old – Daughter of Trevor and Betty Cloud. Leah's second cousin. Joseph's older sister.
- **Joseph Cloud**, 15 years old – Son of Trevor and Betty Cloud. Leah's second cousin. Bonnie's little brother.

Stanton / Glass Family

Arizona Side of the Family
- **Andrew Clark**, 69 years old – Father of Cindy Clark-Stanton. Married to Sandra Howe. Jacob's grandfather and co-owner of Clark and Brown Mining Company.
- **Paul Stanton**, 42 years old – Oldest child of Alvin and Lucille Stanton. Married to Cindy Clark-Stanton.
- **Cindy Clark-Stanton**, 43 years old – Only child of Andrew Clark and Sandra Howe. Lives in Arizona with her husband Paul and two sons.
- **Jacob Stanton**, 17 years old – Oldest son of Paul and Cindy Stanton.
- **Kyle Stanton**, 15 years old – Youngest son of Paul and Cindy Stanton.

Wisconsin Side of the Family
- **Edith Glass**, 94 years old – Aunt of Alvin Stanton. Last of the Glass sisters still living.
- **Alvin Stanton**, 71 years old – Son of George Stanton & Alice Glass (deceased). Married to Lucille Statler. Father of Paul and Evelyn. Jacob's grandfather.
- **Lucille Statler Stanton**, 68 years old – Married to Alvin Stanton. Mother of Paul and Evelyn. Jacob's grandmother.
- **Ron Larsson**, 41 years old – Married to Evelyn. Father of Natalie and Brian.
- **Evelyn Stanton-Larsson**, 40 years old – Daughter of Alvin and Lucille. Married to Ron Larsson. Mother of Natalie and Brian.
- **Natalie Larsson**, 14 years old – Daughter of Ron and Evelyn. Cousin of Jacob Stanton.
- **Brian Larsson**, 10 years old – Son of Ron and Evelyn. Cousin of Jacob Stanton.
- **Charles Stanton**, 39 years old – Nephew of Alvin Stanton. Married to Wendy Mueller. Father of Matt and Nicholas Stanton.

- **Matt Stanton**, 11 years old – Son of Charles Stanton. Cousin of Jacob Stanton.
- **Nicholas (Nickie) Stanton**, 6 years old – Youngest son of Charles Stanton. Cousin of Jacob Stanton.
- **Bobby Cromer**, 45 years old – Husband of Christy Stanton.
- **Christy Stanton Cromer**, 43 years old – Niece of Alvin Stanton and Charles Stanton's sister. Married to Bobby Cromer.
- **Jenny Cromer**, 12 years old – Daughter of Bobby and Christy.

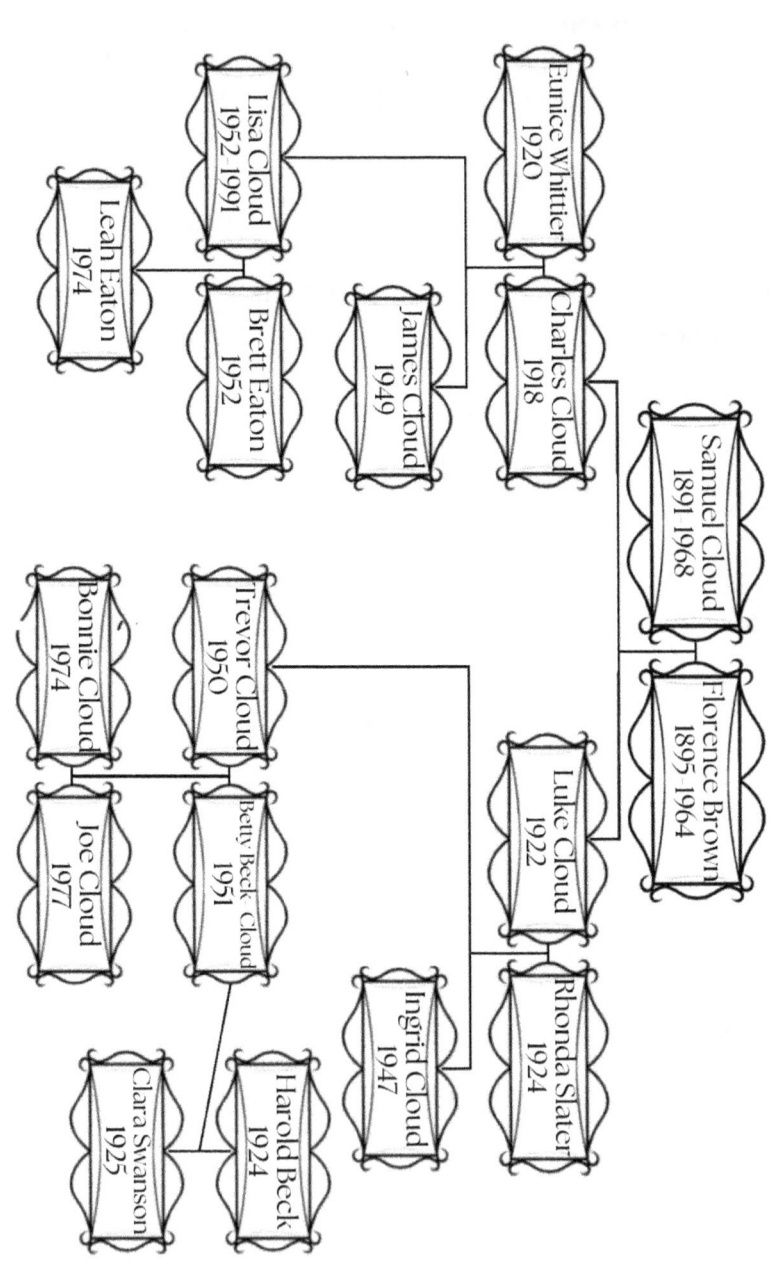

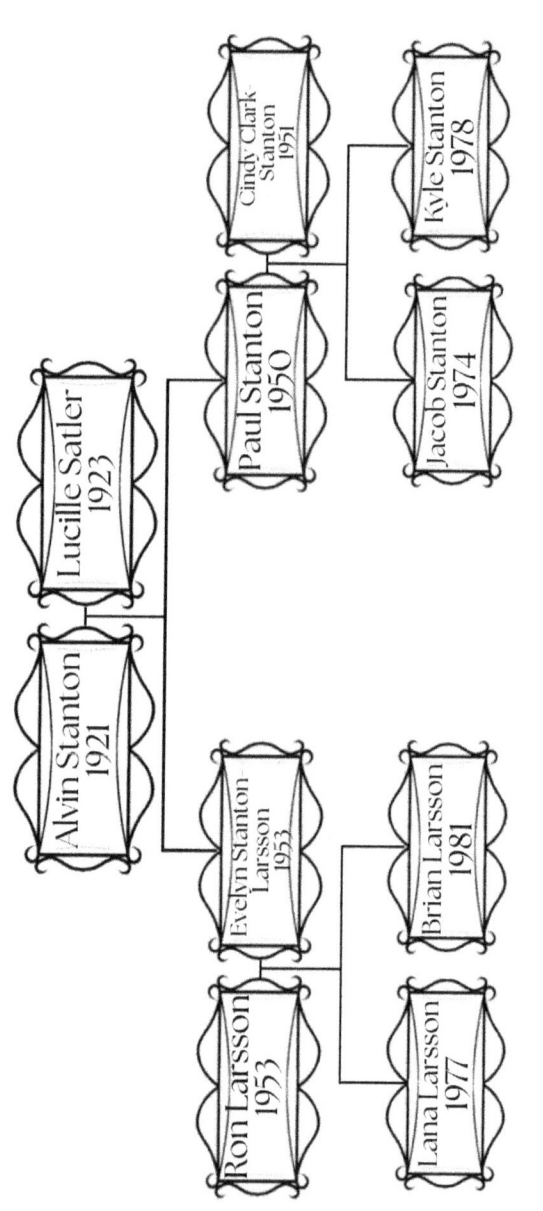

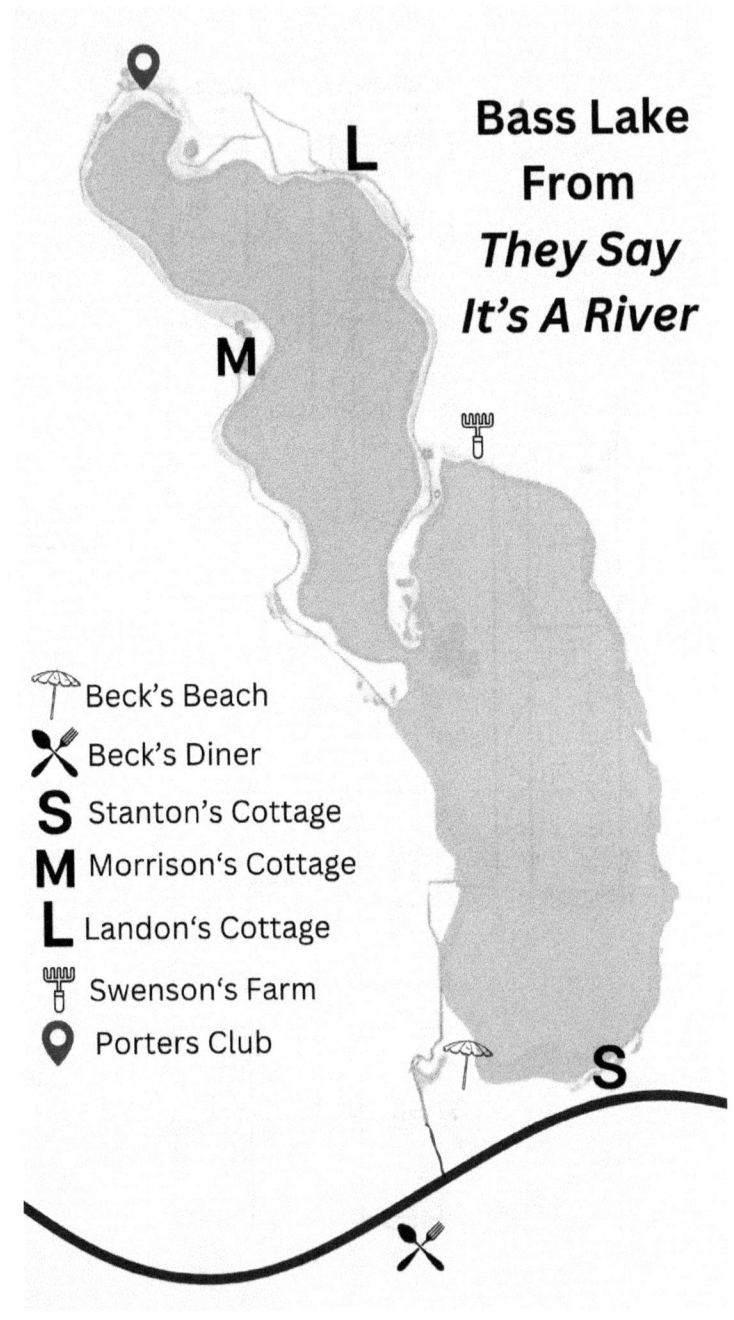

Coming Soon!
Something to Talk About
Love in Laodicea, Book Two

From the screened porch, Evelyn scanned below to the boys eating on the dock, their feet hanging off into the water. Her eyes drifted to the teens' table, noticing Jake facing away from her, but his body language toward the girls speaking for itself.

Like a vulture circling, she walked around the table. "So, what's going on with those two, anyway?" she dryly conferred to Betty.

"I don't know. Those girls talk perpetually, but I'm not party to their conversations," Betty brushed aside her comment. "I do know Jake picked her up yesterday and brought her back, giddy as a schoolgirl and soaked to the bone from the rainstorm."

Evelyn murmured something disparaging into her tea.

"Evelyn, let the boy be." Lucy caught the eye of her daughter. "Give him a little summer crush before his mother steamrolls everything."

"I couldn't agree more." Alvin added to try and change the subject. "I have to say, Trevor, your niece is quite the pistol. She can shoot one-liners faster than a sharpshooter. Is that a family trait?"

"That was her mother's specialty," Trevor replied. "Her tongue could be as sharp as a razor and quick as a whip from her brain. It hurts a little, seeing her, as she is so much like her mom," he finished with a squeeze of Betty's hand.

"Sorry, I didn't mean to bring that up," Alvin grimaced.

"It's okay. I'm so glad we got Leah here for this summer. We're all worried about what's coming next." Treavor confessed.

"And what's that?" Evelyn took a moment away from monitoring the yard.

"Brett's family never attempted to blend with ours. They are born in Texas, live in Texas, and die in Texas. The funeral was the second time in my life that I've ever seen Ethel in person. The first was at their wedding. She tries to control that man's life, with her top attack-dog being his sister, Caroline."

"Really," Lucy was surprised by this tidbit of family gossip.

"I've heard all about it from your mother," Clara continued, trying to confirm with Trevor what she was told. "Did Caroline really try to take charge at the funeral and make changes to what was being done at the service?"

"You heard correctly," Trevor tapped his fingers, remembering the chaos. "That woman is a narcissist on an epic scale. Leah has been fighting with her dad about where they are going to live since she got here. That woman is already trying to put on a mom hat with Leah."

Lucy felt anger within herself. "How do you think that's gonna work?"

"Spend a day with her, and that will answer your question," Alvin lightly elbowed his wife.

"Yeah, but they got him to move," Betty voiced with concern. "About ten years ago, Caroline and Ethel made a full-court press for the family to move to Houston. Brett was told very curtly by Lisa that he was welcome to go to Texas all he wanted, but he would only need to pack a single suitcase."

"Dang," chuckled Alvin. "So that's where she gets it."

"Yup," Trevor laughed. "I hope your grandson knows what he's getting into with that one."

"Well, if there is kryptonite for that boy," Alvin said, peering down at Jake, who was sitting with rapt attention below, "He's currently taken in by a double feature."

"And that is what worries me," Evelyn put down her tea. "Want something stronger, Mom?"

"Now that you mention it, dear, yes. I'll take Bartles and James Orange, please."

As they heard varied talk above them, Natalie turned to Leah.

"So, what do you think they are talking about?" Natalie looked over her shoulder, hearing the chuckles and tell-tale tones of her mother's suspiciousness echoing in her ears.

"Oh, I'm sure you two are high on the list, especially after yesterday." Bonnie zeroed her eyes on the couple.

Natalie dropped her jaw, turning to her cousin. "What did you do?"

"Nothing," Jake replied with as short a tone as he could.

"Really, Jacob?" Leah nudged him with her foot under the table. "Nothing, huh?"

"No, not that it was nothing, Leah," he whispered, trying to play offense and defense on both fields. "I just don't want to get things stirred up."

Natalie mouthed her confusion to Bonnie, "Jacob?"

"You'll get used to it," Bonnie told her as she fake stuck her finger down her throat, making a gagging noise.

"What happened?" Natalie scooted closer.

"We took a walk in the rain and got completely soaked. And it was...very romantic," was Leah's warm reply, running her hand over his across the table.

"Yes," Jake agreed, fading his gaze into hers. "It was."

Bonnie stood up. "I think I'm going to go get something else to drink before I get nauseous. Would you join me, Leah?"

"I could use some more banana pudding," Leah relented to the hint, wondering what Bonnie was wanting to talk about.

As they walked away, Natalie whispered towards her cousin, "So, what happened?"

Jake smirked a goofy grin. "Natalie, I'm not one to kiss and tell, you know that," he winked.

"Oh my gosh, Jacob Ryan Stanton," she covered her mouth.

"Shhh," Jake put his finger to his lips. "I don't need any fire alarms going off over lunch, as your mom has her detector set to high."

In the kitchen, Evelyn, Betty, Clara, and Lucy were in deep conversation.

"I'm still not sold on the idea of him being out here," Evelyn pointed at her mother. "I know he's almost eighteen, but the boy's reputation far precedes him."

"Reputation?" Betty was taken aback.

Lucy placed a hand on her daughter's shoulder, "Evelyn, you gotta take what Cindy tells you with a grain of salt."

"Betty, I believe you should remember Paul quite clearly as a teenager," Evelyn continued with a bit of drip in her voice. "Let me just say, the apple doesn't fall far from the tree."

Betty's expression iced over, "Evelyn, even if I knew what you were trying to infer, I would assure you that I know my niece far..." She stopped as Leah and Bonnie entered the adjacent dining room. "Hey, girls, what are you looking for? We were starting to get things cleaned up for the afternoon."

"More banana pudding, Mom," Bonnie answered, unsure of what to make of the conversation they walked in on.

"Here, just take the container back out with you," Clara handed her the blue Tupperware bowl. "I see your grandfather is up; I'm sure that's what he's looking for."

"What are you girls up to for the afternoon?" asked Betty before Evelyn could say anything else.

"Probably catching up with Krissy at Porter's like I talked about," Bonnie told her mom.

"Sounds like a good idea. Have fun." Betty waved as they headed out.

In the yard, Leah questioned Bonnie on the conversation inside. "So, what was Evelyn talking about with your mom?"

"I'm not entirely sure, but I guarantee they were talking about you and Mr. Clueless over there," Bonnie pointed as they approached Jake and Natalie.

"I'm going to see if Krissy is here yet. I'll be back in a few," Bonnie told them and she headed toward her car.

With tables cleared, Ron helped Natalie navigate the pontoon out of the boathouse and tethered it to the pier as Brian and Joe began getting fishing poles out. Trevor, Alvin, and Harold joined them in rigging up for a short fishing expedition.

The women had settled into the assortment of wicker and adirondack chairs on the lawn, enjoying the afternoon breeze off the lake with their glasses of wine.

About twenty minutes later, the sound and sight of a motorboat came toward the dock, with Krissy at the helm and Bonnie leaning out over the bow, enjoying the spray. As it coasted up to the opposite side of the dock, Trevor took the line his daughter tossed to him and tied the boat up.

Betty looked at her daughter and her friend. "So, what's going on at Porter's tonight?"

"They're having a bonfire and game night. Dylan and Mote are already there," Krissy answered. "I told Bonnie earlier to come over after lunch and we'd take the boat back and pick up Leah and Jake, if that's okay."

"Fine by me," Betty cast a sidelong smile at Evelyn, who just shook her head. "Bonnie, just don't be too late driving back and please watch for deer."

"I will, Mom. Love you," she said as she gave her mom a quick hug. "Bye, everybody."

"Have fun. I'll see you both bright and early," Clara reminded them.

"Don't I know it," Bonnie laughed as she and Leah walked toward the boat.

Jake was talking with his uncle as they loaded the pontoon boat. Leah slid beside him. "Well, are you coming, Jacob?" she lilted with emphasis on 'Jacob.'

"Oh, yeah." He abruptly went to follow her. "Bye. See you later."

Alvin stopped him before he got into the boat, "Have fun," and lowered his voice just enough before he added, "But not too much, so those women don't murder me," he finished, hinting toward the eight pairs of eyes watching intently.

"Don't worry, Grandpa. I'll just be me," Jake patted his shoulder, flashing a broad smile as he scampered into the boat.

Ron felt for the old man, "For your sake, I hope he does, since you're the one who convinced those women that him being here was a good idea."

"Trust me," Alvin groaned, "I've been reminded of that."

Trevor tossed the line back to Bonnie and Krissy began to

hand out life jackets before they pulled away from the dock. Jake settled up in the small bench seat at the bow, facing toward the back of the boat, as Leah cuddled up next to him.

"I don't think your aunt likes me," her eyes voicing her worry as she sat, adjusting the straps.

"Why is that?" Jake turned to face her and put his arm around her so they both could sit comfortably.

"Her and my aunt were having quite a terse conversation that seemed to be about you when Bonnie and I walked into the kitchen."

"Oh, that's just Evelyn. She isn't happy unless she is stirring things up and knee-deep in everybody's business," Jake tried to explain as Krissy started up the motor and slowly backed away from the dock.

"I could tell," Leah spoke into his ear as the boat pulled around and they could see everyone waving. "Well, maybe we should help the situation," she added with a wicked grin.

"Help how?" Jake didn't follow her, as he waved back to the shore.

"Give them something to talk about," Leah said as she pulled Jake in close and kissed him.

A Final Thought

As you close this book, I hope you've been touched by the story. Perhaps you've found yourself reflecting on your own life, your relationships, or seen personal reflections through the eyes of the characters.

Love, as we've explored, is not merely a feeling, it's an action. It's the choice to give of oneself, to put the needs of others before our own. It's the quiet act of kindness, the supportive word, the patient ear.

If you have been moved by the stories within it please share this book with a friend, family member, or someone who could use a little inspiration. Help us continue to touch hearts and inspire more in this cold world to see that the greatest gift is to give.

Acknowledgements

I owe an immense debt to my amazing wife, my sounding board for hundreds of revisions and ideas. With all my heart...for the journey ahead.

To my girls, the sea glass within my life, the beauty that shines through the brokenness.

To my editor, Tweed, and Squill Publishing, thank you for finding the diamonds in the rough, guiding me through the development process, and helping my ideas become the story they are today.

To Angelina Cairo, thank you for your support from the early Wattpad drafts to creating the visualization that has become the cover of this book. Keep exploring your creative dreams.

To my Wattpad followers and fans who inspired new ideas and encouraged me from those early trial chapters to the many reads and comments that precipitated the launching of this book.

To my Discord family, my 7 Crew: Nora, Fiz, Jocie, Gary, Marichat, JP, and Danyell, it takes a village to reach the summit. A special thanks to Hope for your unparalleled support on the Beta draft and counter-insight that helped me hear Bonnie's voice.

To Family: Mom and Dad, thank you for always giving me the space to explore my creativity down the varied paths it took. To my brother and sister-in-law, my thanks for being the hands and feet that, many times, I could not be, and for creating the opportunity to renew my path home. To my aunts, uncles, and cousins, thank you for the memories and enduring the tales I conjured over the years.

To the candle on my water, whose light burned out far too soon, may the spark you started shine through the words within.

To Mary, who lived the golden rule as a path for us to follow, long after your passing.

And to my Savior, who has brought within my life glimpses of pure love and the definition of Love given away.

JM grew up under the sunny skies of Arizona but spent his summers exploring the lake country of Wisconsin. There, he discovered his love for fishing, boating, and the great outdoors. Now living in Central Ohio with his wife and five daughters, JM enjoys exploring the Midwest, attending theater performances, and spending time with their menagerie of cats and two dogs—including their lovable pug, Maggie.

www.ingramcontent.com/pod-product-compliance
Lightning Source LLC
Chambersburg PA
CBHW071213090426
42736CB00014B/2802